Easy Guide to Attachment Disorders in Adults

Understanding adult attachment styles and relationships and attachment trauma and healing

Vanessa Alvarez

CANTONFIELD PUBLISHING

Contents

Chapter 1

What is attachment disorder in adults?

Attachment disorder is a psychological condition characterized by problems in forming close relationships and maintaining them. It is defined as a disturbance in the development of emotional bonds with people who are significant to you. The term "attachment" refers to your relationship with someone else, such as family members, friends, teachers, caregivers and others.

Attachment disorders are caused by inadequate caretaking during childhood. They include avoidant attachment disorder, anxious/ambivalent attachment disorder, and disorganized attachment disorder. These conditions cause problems forming secure attachments with others. Insecure attachments lead to poor self-esteem, anxiety, depression, and low self-efficacy.

Different attachment styles affect our ability form healthy relationships. We tend to fall into one of three different categories: secure, insecure-avoidant, and insecure-anxious. Secure people feel safe and confident around others. Avoidants do not want to get too close to anyone because they fear being hurt again. Anxiously attached people seek reassurance and attention from others. Disorganized people experience intense distress when separated from caregivers.

The cause of this disorder is unknown. However, some researchers believe that the way parents treat their children plays a role in whether or not a child develops AD. If a parent is inconsistent in his or her parenting style, then the child may develop AD. Other factors that contribute to developing AD include abuse during childhood, neglect, parental separation, divorce, and mental health issues.

The fundamentals: Attachment theory

Attachment theory was developed by John Bowlby in 1969. It explains how children develop relationships with their parents and caregivers. The theory states that humans attach themselves to people who they feel safe with, whom they trust, and whose behavior resembles their own. In this way, we learn to understand ourselves through our experiences with others.

Bowlby believed that attachment patterns were formed during infancy and childhood, and that these patterns continued into adulthood. He thought that adults could change their attachment behaviors if they knew what caused them. He considered his theories to be universal, which means that they apply across cultures and genders. However, some researchers believe that there are cultural differences in attachment behaviors. For example, Western culture emphasizes individuality and self-reliance, whereas Eastern culture values collectivism and interdependence.

Attachment theory explains how children develop emotional bonds with caregivers. When those early experiences aren't positive, it affects how we relate to our partners later in life.

Insecure attachment styles include avoidant, resistant, anxious/ambivalent, and disorganized.

Securely attached people feel safe around others and trust them. They're comfortable being close to others.

An avoidant person avoids closeness because he or she fears getting hurt. A resistant person resists closeness because he or her needs aren't met.

People with anxious/ambivalent styles experience anxiety about intimacy. They don't know what to do or say.

Disorganized people have trouble organizing things into categories and sequences. This leads to problems with organization and planning.

Types of attachment disorder

There are two types of attachment disorder according to DSM5. One involves children who experience insecure attachments during childhood. These children tend to develop anxiety about closeness due to experiences that caused them fear or pain. They may become fearful of being close to people because they experienced rejection or abandonment. This form of attachment disorder tends to occur in young children.

The second type of attachment disorder occurs later in life. People with this disorder typically had secure attachments as infants and toddlers. However, during adolescence and adulthood, they begin to withdraw from relationships. They may feel anxious around loved ones and avoid intimacy.

Avoidant attachment disorder occurs when a child avoids any closeness with her mother or father because she fears rejection. She may feel anxious if she is away from her parents. She may become angry at them if they try to comfort her. Avoidant children often do not want to play with others and prefer to stay alone. They may seem shy or withdrawn around strangers. Some children who suffer from this disorder grow up to be adults who rarely show affection toward anyone except family members.

Resistant attachment disorder occurs when a baby cries when he wants something and refuses to take care of himself. He may refuse to eat unless someone feeds him. He may throw tantrums when he doesn't get what he wants. His behavior may be aggressive or passive. A child with this type of disorder may cry inconsolably, scream loudly, hit, kick, bite, scratch, or even hurt himself accidentally. This kind of attachment disorder usually goes away by itself without treatment. However, some children with this disorder continue to act out after they reach adulthood.

Disordered attachment disorder occurs when a person's emotions are so intense that he cannot control them. For example, he might yell, scream, or lash out against people who don't understand him. When he is upset, he may punch walls or break things. People who suffer from this disorder may also have trouble sleeping. It is very rare for a person to have only one form of attachment disorder. Most people have several forms of attachment disorders.

Reactive attachment disorder

RAD is an extreme form of Disorganized Attachment Disorder (DAD). DAD is one of the most common forms of childhood trauma. In fact, it affects up to 10% of children worldwide. This is why we are calling on parents, teachers and professionals working with young people to raise awareness of RAD.

Reactive Attachment Disorder (or RAD) is a condition where children do not develop normal social skills and relationships due to early trauma. It is characterized by problems with emotional regulation, impulse control, anger management, anxiety, depression, self-esteem, and peer relations. The symptoms usually start before age 5 years old and last until adolescence.

The term "attachment" refers to the way people relate to others. In this case, the word attachment means how a child relates to his/her parents. Adults who suffer from RAD show signs of having been neglected or abused when they were young. This causes them to form attachments to their caregivers rather than forming healthy relationships with peers.

Adults with RAD often feel anxious around new people, especially if they are unfamiliar. They may become aggressive towards strangers or even violent. They may act out aggressively against other kids at school or home. They may get into fights with siblings or friends. If left untreated, these behaviors could lead to serious consequences such as suicide attempts, substance abuse, and violence.

Symptoms of Reactive Attachment Disorder in Adults

Reactive attachment disorder is a type of childhood trauma that affects children during infancy and early childhood. This trauma causes lasting emotional damage, often leading to symptoms such as anxiety, depression, substance abuse and self-harm. In some cases, it leads to reactive attachment disorder in adults.

RAD is characterized by a pattern of behavior that occurs over months or even years. People suffering from RAD are unable to form healthy relationships because they don't understand how others feel and react. They tend to become angry easily and lash out without thinking about the consequences. They may withdraw from social situations, avoid eye contact and prefer solitude.

The good news is that treatment is possible. A combination of psychotherapy, medication and support from friends and family can help people overcome their issues.

Disinhibited social engagement disorder

A new study published in the Journal of Psychiatric Research found that those diagnosed with Disinhibited Social Engagements Disorder (DSED) had fewer friends and less family support than those without the diagnosis. The researchers used data collected from the National Epidemiologic

Survey on Alcohol and Related Conditions (NESARC), a survey conducted every four years since 2001. In NESARC, participants answered questions regarding alcohol use, drug abuse, mental health problems, and physical health conditions. They also completed questionnaires designed to measure personality traits.

The researchers analyzed responses from 10,814 adults aged 18 and older who participated in NESARC. Of those, 4,926 met criteria for DSM-5 disorders, including 2,741 cases of Disordered Social Engagement (DSED). Compared to those without DSED, individuals with DSED reported lower levels of self-esteem, less satisfaction with life, and more symptoms of anxiety and depression.

The Prevalence Of Attachment Disorder In Adults

Attachment disorder is often overlooked in adults because it can go undiagnosed for decades. A study published in the Journal of Clinical Psychiatry found that attachment disorders are prevalent among adult patients seeking treatment. Researchers looked at data from over 2,500 people ages 18 to 65 who sought help for anxiety or depression at one of four clinics around the United States. They discovered that about 5% of those surveyed had been diagnosed with some form of attachment disorder.

According to Dr. Michael J. Poulin, a psychiatrist at Massachusetts General Hospital, there are three main types of attachment disorders: insecure-avoidant, secure base anxious, and disorganized/disoriented. Secure base anxious refers to someone who fears abandonment and seeks reassurance from others. Disorganized/disoriented describes someone who doesn't know how to relate to others. An example of this might be someone who struggles with social skills and becomes easily overwhelmed.

Insecure avoidant individuals tend to feel uncomfortable being alone and seek out relationships even though they're afraid of rejection. This type of person tends to be clingy and overly dependent on others.

How Attachment Styles Affect Adult Relationships

Your attachment style affects every aspect—from how you form friendships to how you date. If you struggle with insecurity, it can affect everything from your romantic relationships to your ability to build meaningful connections. Understanding your attachment style can help you understand why you feel insecure and what you might do differently to improve your relationship skills.

Attachment theory suggests that we are born with certain ways of relating to others. These patterns of interaction are called attachment styles. We develop our attachment styles based on early experiences with caregivers. For example, someone who was neglected or abused during childhood may grow up feeling unsafe and anxious around people. This person may become very dependent on his or her partner and unable to trust anyone else.

If you find yourself struggling to make friends, dating, or building strong relationships, you could have an insecure attachment style. You may be afraid of being abandoned again, or worried about whether your partner will like you. Or maybe you grew up in a family where everyone seemed to love each other except for you. As a child, you may have felt left out, unloved, or even jealous of those who got attention while you didn't.

Insecurity is normal. But if you don't know how your attachment style affects your relationships, you won't be able to change it.

Related Conditions

Attachment disorders affect how children learn about relationships with others. They impact how children form attachments with caregivers and peers. This impacts how they behave toward others and themselves. In addition, children with attachment disorders often experience other mental health issues such as depression, anxiety, self-harm, eating disorders, substance abuse, and suicidal thoughts.

For example, children with insecure attachment styles tend to feel anxious around people they don't know well. They are less likely to trust strangers and show fear when someone tries to hurt them. As a result, they might avoid certain situations or become aggressive towards others.

Is It Possible to Change My Attachment Style?

Attachment theory says we learn how to relate to people based on our early experiences. Those experiences shape our beliefs about what it takes to make a relationship work — or fail. If you grew up with parents who weren't emotionally available, you might believe that intimacy requires constant reassurance. And if you had a parent who was physically abusive, you might think that love involves being controlled and dominated.

If you grew up with parents like those, it makes sense that you'd end up feeling anxious around romantic partners. You might find yourself constantly worrying about whether someone will hurt you or abandon you. Or you might fear that if you let down your guard, he'll reject you.

But while there's no way to change your genes, you can change your behavior. In fact, research suggests that changing your behaviors can help you overcome some of the negative effects of childhood trauma. Here are five ways to improve your ability to build meaningful relationships:

1. Practice mindfulness. Mindfulness helps you become aware of your thoughts and feelings without getting caught up in them. When you practice mindfulness, you focus on the present moment, rather than thinking about the past or anticipating the future. This lets you notice the

things happening right now, such as your breathing or the sensation of touching something.

2. Accept yourself. While you shouldn't try to change who you are, you do need to accept yourself. For example, if you've been raised in an environment where you felt ashamed of your body, you probably won't feel comfortable showing off your curves. But if you accept yourself just the way you are, you'll be able to connect better with others.

3. Be patient. If you grew up in an environment where you didn't receive much emotional support, it's easy to assume that everyone else does too. So when you meet someone who seems needy or clingy, you might automatically say "no thanks." But if you're willing to give someone space, you could discover that they really are looking for connection.

4. Trust your gut. As children, we learned to rely on our instincts because our survival depended on it. Nowadays, many of us still follow our intuition, even though we know it isn't always reliable. To develop healthier relationships, you need to start trusting your instincts again. Ask yourself questions like: Do I feel safe with this person? Does she seem trustworthy? Is she giving me

enough attention? How does she treat her friends?

5. Take risks. Sometimes, you have to take chances to get closer to other people. That doesn't mean you should jump into bed with anyone who asks. Instead, ask yourself: What would happen if I did this? Would I regret it later? Could I handle rejection? If you answer yes to any of these questions, then go ahead and try it out.

Attachment-Based Therapy for Adults

Attachment-based therapy helps adults work through issues related to childhood traumas. Patients are encouraged to examine how they attach to others and themselves. This process allows them to learn about their early experiences and develop coping strategies. They learn to identify and change behaviors that cause distress.

The goal of treatment is to help clients develop healthy attachments and improve overall well-being.

In order to understand the effects of attachment styles on adult life, it is important to know what happens to children who grow up without stable parental figures. Insecurely attached children tend to be highly dependent on their caregivers. They usually lack confidence in their own abilities and skills.

If you want to use attachment theory to help your life, here are some suggestions:

1) Write down your earliest memories and describe them in detail. Draw pictures to illustrate the memories you remember best.

2) Think back to your first grade teacher. Describe her personality, mannerisms, and behaviors. Write down everything you remember about her.

3) Look at a photo album from your childhood. Describe each picture in detail.

4) Talk to your parents about your childhood. Ask them about their relationship with you.

How to Help a Partner With an Attachment Disorder

When we think about people with attachment disorders, we tend to think of children with parents who are unavailable emotionally. We think of adults whose partners don't show up for work, don't pay attention to them, or simply disappear without explanation. But there are many different types of attachment disorders. Some involve children; some involve adults; some affect both. And most aren't caused by one specific event. They're a lifelong struggle.

The good news is that attachment disorders are treatable. You can learn ways to understand and support your partner, even if she won't admit her problems. If you've ever been involved with someone with an attachment disorder—and I'm talking about those who suffer from borderline personality disorder, narcissistic personality disorder, avoidant personality disorder, and histrionic personality disorder—you know that it takes patience and understanding to help him/her.

Here are tips for helping someone with an attachment disorder.

1. Understand What Your Partner Is Going Through

People with attachment disorders experience emotional pain differently than others do. For example, they might feel anger, sadness, fear, or anxiety, but they don't necessarily express those feelings outwardly. Instead, they might become withdrawn, depressed, or irritable. They may act like everything is fine, but underneath the surface, they're suffering.

2. Know How to Recognize Signs of Attachment Disorders

If you notice signs of an attachment disorder in your partner, look for the following behaviors:

- He/she has difficulty trusting other people.
- He/she avoids relationships because he/she feels unsafe.
- She/he becomes angry when things don't go his/her way.
- He/She doesn't seem interested in sex.
- He/He spends too much time alone.
- He/s talks about suicide.

3. Be Patient

It's hard to watch someone you love struggle with an attachment disorder. It's also difficult to accept that your partner isn't going to change overnight. However, you have to keep in mind that this person needs time to heal. Don't expect immediate results. Give him/her space to come out of his/her shell.

4. Encourage Him/Her to Seek Professional Help

Your partner may not be able to get professional help on his/her own. That's why you need to encourage him/her to seek treatment. The sooner he/she gets help, the better.

5. Stay Positive

You can't control what happens to your partner, but you can control how you react to it. Try to stay positive. Remember that your partner will eventually recover.

Chapter 2

Attachment styles

Attachment theory says that people can fall into one of three categories based on how they relate to others. There are those who are securely attached, those who are insecurely attached, and those who are avoidantly attached.

Securely attached individuals are comfortable with intimacy and enjoy having strong connections with others. These people are confident about their ability to make friends and maintain friendships. They are able to establish healthy relationships with others.

Insecurely attached individuals struggle with trusting others because they fear rejection. They are sensitive to criticism and are hesitant to show affection out of concern that it might be misinterpreted. They are less likely to seek social support and may even avoid seeking help when needed.

Avoidantly attached individuals are wary of getting too close to others. They rarely initiate contact and are reluctant to express feelings. They may seem aloof and distant, but they are actually just trying to protect themselves from potential hurt.

There are four adult attachment styles:

Attachment theory says that we learn how to relate to others based on our experiences growing up. If you grew up in a secure environment where you felt safe and loved, you learned to trust yourself and others. You know what it feels like to be rejected and to experience love and affection.

If you grew up in a less secure environment, you learned to rely on yourself and others to protect you. You developed strategies to deal with anxiety and uncertainty.

A person with an anxious attachment style tends to seek out reassurance and approval from others. They want to be told that everything is okay even though they don't really believe it.

People with an avoidant attachment style try to hide themselves away. They do not want to show anyone that they care because they think they'll be hurt.

Secure people enjoy being around others and enjoy sharing their feelings. They realize that everyone makes mistakes and that no one is perfect.

The most common type of attachment style is called "secure." This is the best way to describe someone who is comfortable with his or her own emotions and does not worry too much about whether he or she gets along with others.

The next most common type of attachment is called "avoidant," which describes someone who avoids emotional connections. He or she fears rejection and tries to keep distance from others.

Finally, there is "disorganized/anxious." These people struggle to form healthy attachments and sometimes become overwhelmed by strong emotions. They may act impulsively and lash out when they are angry or afraid.

Anxious / Preoccupied

Anxious attachment is characterized by a fear of separation and loss. This type of attachment style causes people to become preoccupied with thoughts about being abandoned or rejected. If you experience this type of attachment, you may find yourself clinging to your partner, feeling insecure, and worrying about whether your partner will abandon you. You may also be overly dependent on your partner, demanding constant reassurance.

It is considered one of three styles of attachment, along with secure and avoidant attachment. It is associated with insecurely attached children who lack a sense of security and safety in their relationships with caregivers. A child who experiences this kind of attachment tends to become preoccupied with fears of separation and loss, and often becomes clingy and fearful of losing the person he loves most. This type of attachment pattern is common among those who suffer from depression, anxiety disorders, eating disorders, substance abuse, etc.

The difference between secure and dismissing attachment styles is that secure individuals generally do not worry excessively about their relationship with others. Dismissing parents usually provide little emotional support to their children, and they may even reject their child's attempts at intimacy. In contrast, secure adults typically trust themselves and others, and they enjoy close relationships. People who were rejected by their primary caregivers as infants tend to develop insecure attachments because they did not receive enough love and attention from their mothers and fathers. When these individuals grow up, they may find themselves unable to form healthy romantic relationships.

Insecure attachment patterns are thought to play a role in the development of these mental health problems. For example, research suggests that insecure attachment is linked to increased symptoms of depression and anxiety, and decreased self-esteem. In addition, studies suggest that insecure attachment patterns predict poor treatment outcomes for patients with mood disorders.

Avoidant / Dismissive

Avoidant/dismissal attachment styles are characterized by avoidance of closeness and dependence, and fear of abandonment and rejection. People who have this type of attachment tend to keep their distance from others and prefer independence and autonomy. They often feel anxious when they become close to someone else because they worry that they might lose control over themselves if they depend too much on another person. In addition, people with avoidant attachment tend to believe that relationships are difficult and unpredictable. They don't like to share feelings and thoughts with others and try to protect themselves from emotional pain.

People with avoidant attachment styles are often described as being cold and unemotional. They don't want to depend on others because they fear rejection and abandonment. This makes it difficult for people with avoidant attachment styles to form relationships with others. In fact, adults with avoidant attachment styles often have a negative view of their own abilities and talents. As a result, they feel like failures and worry about what others think of them.

The term "avoidant" refers to a general tendency to avoid intimacy and dependency. The term "dismissive" means rejecting and distancing oneself from others. Some individuals use these behaviors to cope with painful emotions. Others use them to help them deal with interpersonal problems. For example, some people avoidant of intimacy and rejections may engage in self-destructive behavior such as drug abuse or eating disorders. Those who dismiss others may use aggressive behavior to make themselves feel powerful and invulnerable.

People with avoidant attachment tend not to trust others and do not want to get involved in intimate relationships. They usually have difficulty maintaining friendships and maintain few romantic attachments.

The good news is that you can learn how to overcome your fears and build healthy relationships. You just need to understand where your style came from.

Secure Attachment

Insecure attachment styles are characterized as being unable to develop trusting relationships. This is because we have trouble depending on others and feeling safe in our relationships. We tend to think about how much we care about someone else, rather than thinking about what makes us happy together. An insecure attachment style prevents us from forming strong bonds with others.

People who are securely attached can rely on their partners, while those with an avoidant attachment cannot trust others. A secure attachment style allows you to feel safe in your relationship. You don't worry too much about whether you'll find love again, because you know that you're going to be able to count on your partner.

Securely attached individuals are likely to form stronger attachments to their children than those with an anxious attachment style. They enjoy spending quality time with their kids, and they are more likely to make sure their kids' needs are met.

Disorganized attachment styles develop due early life experiences. Children who grow up without sufficient care tend to develop an anxious attachment style. This happens because they experience frequent changes in caregivers and do not know what to expect next. As a consequence, they become confused and disoriented.

The history of attachment theory research.

Attachment theory was originally developed by John Bowlby. His idea was that children learn how to relate to others based on their experiences with caregivers. He believed that people form secure bonds with their parents early in life, while those who experience abuse or neglect tend to form insecure attachments later in life.

Mary Ainsworth expanded on his ideas by developing the concept of "attachment behaviors," which she observed in her studies of infants and toddlers. She found that there are three types of attachment behaviors: secure, avoidant and resistant. Securely attached individuals seek out and maintain close relationships with their caretakers. Avoidantly attached individuals try to keep away from their caretakers, and resistively attached individuals actively fight against being cared for.

In the 1980s, researchers began studying adults' attachment styles. They discovered that people who had been abused as children tended to have insecure attachment patterns. These individuals experienced trauma as children, and formed negative attitudes toward themselves and others. For example, they might blame themselves for their parent's death, or feel guilty about having survived.

People who grow up in abusive homes often develop insecure attachments. This happens because their caregivers don't provide enough emotional support, or they're too overprotective. As a result, the child develops a fear of closeness, and struggles to build healthy relationships throughout adulthood.

How attachment styles are formed.

Attachment theory is one of the most influential theories in psychology. It explains why we form close bonds with certain people and why those bonds are often broken. Insecure attachment patterns are thought to contribute to many mental health issues such as depression and anxiety.

Secure attachment is typically associated with healthy outcomes, while fearfulavoidance attachment tends toward negative ones, anxious attachment is linked to depression, and avoidant attachment is related to anxieties.

The concept of attachment is rooted in childhood development. Children learn about themselves and others through interactions with primary caretakers. These early experiences shape how adults relate to each other later in life.

Infidelity can cause insecurity in romantic relationships. People who experience infidelity tend to feel insecure in their current relationship. They might question whether their partner still loves them or whether he or she could ever betray them again. This insecurity can lead to feelings of rejection and abandonment.

Can your attachment style change?

Attachment theory says that our earliest experiences shape how we relate to others throughout life. Securely attached individuals learn to trust others and feel safe around them. They rely on those close to them for support, comfort and guidance.

Insecure people, however, don't feel safe enough to depend on anyone else. They fear rejection and abandonment, and seek out partners who won't hurt them. When things go wrong, insecure people blame themselves for being inadequate.

The good news is that you can change your attachment style—and it doesn't take a therapist to do it. You just need to understand what makes you tick. Here are four steps to help you figure out whether you're securely attached or insecurely attached:

1. Ask yourself some questions about your childhood. What did you experience growing up? Were there times when you felt unsafe, lonely or rejected? Did you receive consistent love and affection from your parents? If not, ask yourself why. Was there someone in your family who showed you unconditional love? How did he or she treat you?

2. Think about your current romantic relationship. Do you feel comfortable sharing your feelings with your partner? Are you able to talk openly about problems without feeling judged? Does your partner show interest in your opinions and ideas?

3. Take a look at your personality type. Your personality type describes the way you think, act and react. Is your personality compatible with your partner's? Or does your partner seem like a stranger to you?

4. Finally, consider your parenting style. Do you believe in discipline, limit setting and rules? Do you encourage independence and self-reliance? Or do you prefer to give children freedom and let them make their own decisions?

Get in touch with your real needs.

Avoidant people tend to focus on what others think of them rather than how they feel. This causes them to ignore their inner voice and become disconnected from themselves. As a result, they are unable to express their true desires and needs.

To overcome this problem, you must learn to listen to yourself. You must take care of your emotional health.

You must start taking responsibility for your life.

The most important thing is to accept yourself.

If you do this, you'll find out what really matters to you. And once you know what truly matters to you, you'll be able to make decisions based on those values.

This is one of the biggest challenges of being an avoidant person.

Don't be afraid to seek therapy.

Therapy helps individuals work through issues, develop new skills, and improve relationships. It can help people understand themselves and others better and learn how to talk about emotions. In addition to providing support, therapists can help you cope with anxiety or depression. If you are struggling with stress, depression, anger management, relationship problems, grief, trauma, or addiction, there are many ways to find a therapist. Here are some tips to make sure you choose the best one for you.

1. Ask friends, family members, coworkers, clergy, teachers, coaches, and anyone else you trust for recommendations.

2. Check out online resources like Psychology Today, PsychCentral, and MentalHelp.org. You can also ask your doctor, psychiatrist, psychologist, counselor, social worker, or mental health professional for referrals.

3. Consider asking your insurance provider for a list of providers in your area. Many insurers offer free lists of professionals who accept their plans.

4. Look up "therapist near me" on Yelp.com or Google Local.

5. Visit local clinics and hospitals. Some offer counseling services. Others provide group sessions or individual treatment.

6. Find a therapist who specializes in your problem. For example, if you're having trouble talking to someone about your feelings, look for a therapist who works with couples. Or if you're dealing with depression, consider finding a therapist who specializes in treating it.

Chapter 3

Adult attachment disorder and family conflict

Adult Attachment Issues

Attachment theory suggests that children form attachments to people in their lives. These relationships affect how we view ourselves and others, our sense of self-worth, and even our ability to trust. If you don't feel safe enough to open yourself up to another person, it's harder to build healthy relationships later in life.

The three types of attachment styles are secure, insecure-avoidant, and insecure-ambivalent. You might think that having a secure attachment style makes you less vulnerable to anxiety and depression, but research shows that those who grew up without an attached parent are more likely to experience these mental health problems as adults.

If you're struggling with adult attachment issues, talk therapy is the best treatment option. A therapist can help you understand why you've developed certain behaviors and teach you skills to deal with stressful situations.

Cost of Growing up in Dysfunctional Family

Growing up in a dysfunctional family is tough. Not only do you deal with the emotional trauma of being raised by people who are incapable of loving you properly, but you also have to deal with the fact that you're surrounded by people who don't care about you. You might even go out into the world and find yourself struggling just to survive because no one cares enough to help you. If you ever wanted to understand why some people fail to live happy lives, it helps to consider the impact of growing up in a dysfunctional family.

The cost of growing up in a dysfunctional family is high. But there are ways to avoid the damage done by living in a dysfunctional household.

Personality Disorder in Family Members

Attachment disorders are often associated with other mental health issues. Children who suffer from attachment disorders may display signs of psychopathology later in life. There is no clear link between attachment disorders and antisocial personality disorder. This study examined the prevalence of attachment disorders among family members of children diagnosed with disordered attachment behavior. A total of 595 participants completed an online survey about their child's attachment behaviors and attachment history. Results indicated that approximately one third (34%) of respondents reported having an attachment disorder relating to their child. However, there was no significant difference in the rates of attachment disorders between those who parented a child with attachment problems and those who parented a healthy child.

The Strict Controlling and or Authoritarian Parent

Authoritarian parents are often criticized for being too harsh with their children. They demand obedience and punish disobedience. Authoritarians believe that rules must be followed without question. They enforce discipline harshly and don't allow room for mistakes. They want their kids to do well academically, athletically, socially, etc., and they don't tolerate failure.

Children raised by authoritarian parents tend to become adults who value authority over reason. They're usually very obedient and follow rules unquestioningly. They see themselves as superior to others because they've been given special privileges. And they think it's perfectly acceptable to use power to control others.

When you raise a child with an authoritative parenting style, s/he learns early on how to behave. You teach her/him that there are certain things she/he cannot do. S/He learns to obey rules and follow directions. She/he learns to respect authority figures.

But children who grow up under an authoritative parenting style tend to develop feelings of entitlement. They believe they deserve certain things simply because they exist. They think they're better than everyone else. They don't accept criticism or blame. And they don't understand why they aren't allowed to do something.

If you grew up with an authoritarian parenting style, chances are you learned to treat people poorly. You might even find yourself treating others badly today. But you probably didn't learn to abuse power. You just thought you deserved special treatment.

The Soft Parent

Family systems theory helps us understand why some people develop substance use disorders while others don't. In fact, many people think it's just about "them," whether you're addicted or not. But research shows that family members actually play a significant role in recovery. And family therapy can help family members improve communication skills and learn to work together. This makes sense because we know that families with an SUD are more likely to experience stress and conflict. In turn, this leads to feelings of isolation and helplessness. These emotions make it harder for people to seek treatment. So, family therapy can help family systems become healthier and stronger.

Insecure Nature of Family Attachments

When there are many negative signs in a dysfunctional families, primary care physicians (PCPs) should take immediate actions. In fact, it is better to intervene early rather than later.

A dysfunctional family needs immediate intervention because the emotional distance between parents and children lead to many emotional disorders in young people. Children feel anxious about disapproval, fear anger, and avoid conflicts. They tend to feel guilty when taking responsibility for themselves. They also try to blame others for their own problems. They cannot express their children's feelings clearly. They do not want to deal with closeness and relationships with partners. They often have impulsive behaviors and lack self control. They tend to get into trouble and fail to follow through with tasks well.

Large and Extended Families

Family Systems Theory is a way of understanding human behavior and interaction. This section explores some of the basics behind family systems theory. The concept of family systems theory is based on the idea that people are influenced by the relationships around them. People tend to behave similarly to those closest to them. As we move away from our immediate family, we begin to act differently. We see different things, hear different things, and learn different things. These differences influence our behaviors and attitudes.

Impact of Parental Substance Abuse on Children

Attachment disorders are associated with parent-child relationships characterized by frequent conflict and rejection. This occurs because the child lacks secure attachment to his/her parents. Research suggests that early intervention programs can help improve outcomes for children affected by attachment disorder. However, there is limited research regarding the impact of parental substance use on children. One study found that prenatally exposed infants had lower IQ scores compared to unexposed infants. Another study showed that prenatal cocaine exposure resulted in poorer language skills among preschoolers. Both studies suggest that in utero exposure to drugs impacts brain development.

Early identification of parental substance abuse and treatment is important to prevent later adverse effects on children. A recent review article identified four areas where interventions could be used to address parental substance abuse: parenting education, family therapy, individual counseling, and pharmacotherapy. These strategies can reduce risk factors for drug use and increase protective factors such as social support and self-esteem.

The Impact of Substance Abuse on Parents of Adult Children

Parents are often torn over whether or not to enable their child who struggles with substance abuse. Some believe it is their responsibility to help their addicted child, while others feel helpless because they don't know what to do. This section explores the impact of substance abuse on families, including the role of enabling, and offers suggestions for coping with the problem.

Children with an attachment disorder may exhibit certain characteristics. For example, they may have difficulty regulating emotions, be overly dependent on caregivers, and have poor impulse control. In addition, they may experience anxiety and depression. Researchers have developed a model called the "secure base" which helps explain how these symptoms occur. Securely attached children have a strong sense of security and

Parenting a child with attachment issues

Attachment disorders are common among children and adolescents. These conditions include insecure-avoidant attachment disorder, avoidant attachment disorder, ambivalent attachment disorder, disorganized/disoriented attachment disorder, and unresolved trauma. Children with attachment disorders tend to experience emotional distress, anxiety, depression, behavioral disturbances, and academic underachievement. They may also exhibit aggression toward others or self-destructive behavior.

Parents play a critical role in helping their children develop secure attachments. If parents provide consistent, sensitive, and responsive caregiving throughout childhood, it helps prevent attachment disorders in later life. However, parenting a child with attachment difficulties requires patience and understanding. You must learn how to deal with your own feelings and emotions, while trying to understand what your child is experiencing.

If you suspect your child has an attachment disorder, seek professional help. Your pediatrician, mental health provider, school counselor, social worker, or psychologist can help identify the problem and offer treatment options.

Making a child with an attachment disorder feel secure

Children with attachment disorders are often fearful of being abandoned and don't trust others. They may become clingy and anxious around strangers and avoid social situations. A parent with an attachment disorder may find it difficult to read their children's emotions and respond appropriately.

Set consistent, loving boundaries and keep them consistent. When you set limits, make sure they're realistic and age appropriate. For example, a young toddler might need to eat dinner alone while his parents work late, but he won't understand why his parents aren't home.

Don't react emotionally when your child behaves badly. Instead, try to remain calm and help him learn how to control himself. If you do lose your temper, apologize immediately and let your child know what happened.

Try to maintain predictable routines and schedules. This helps children develop a sense of security.

Own up to mistakes and initiate repair. Your child needs to see you take responsibility for things that go wrong. You can start by apologizing and admitting that you messed up. Then explain how you plan to prevent similar problems in the future. Finally, ask your child how he feels about what happened.

Try not to overreact when your child misbehaves. If you do, you could reinforce his negative behavior and make matters worse. Letting your child know that you're disappointed in him will give him permission to change his ways.

Repairing attachment disorders by helping your child feel loved

Attachment disorders are common among children who grow up without a secure base of support. These kids often struggle to form close friendships and maintain healthy romantic relationships. In fact, research suggests that children with attachment disorders tend to experience difficulties forming lasting attachments with others. One reason for this could be that they do not learn how to regulate their emotions. They may become easily upset and frustrated, especially when they lack attention from caregivers. This makes it difficult for them to trust people.

Children who suffer from attachment disorders often show signs of insecurity. For example, they might cry when left alone, or avoid eye contact with strangers. They may also display behaviors such as clinging, tantrums, and aggression towards themselves or others. If you notice these symptoms in your child, talk to him/her about his/her feelings. You can encourage your child to express himself/herself clearly, and ask questions about what he/she wants. By doing this, you will help him/her understand his/her own thoughts and feelings.

You can also teach your child how to manage his/her stress levels. Children who are stressed out may act aggressively toward themselves and others. To prevent this, explain to your child that being angry doesn't solve anything. Instead, try to find ways to calm down. Take deep breaths, count backwards from 10, or use relaxation techniques like yoga.

If your child still struggles to make friends, consider enrolling him/her in a social skills group. Such groups provide opportunities to practice social skills and build confidence. Also, make sure your child gets plenty of sleep each night. Lack of sleep can cause irritability, which may lead to aggressive behavior.

Finally, give your child lots of hugs and kisses. Showing your child that you care about him/her helps him/her feel safe and secure.

Chapter 4

How attachment disorders can be serious

Is there a link with dissociative identity disorder?

Attachment disorders are characterized by problems forming close relationships with others. They affect how people feel about themselves, their ability to trust others, and how well they cope with stress. Dissociative Identity Disorder (DID), sometimes called Multiple Personality Disorder, is one type of attachment disorder.

There are different types of DID. Some people experience multiple personalities while others do not. A person with DID may switch among several identities. These identities may be separate from each other, or they may be related to each other.

People with DID often suffer from major depression and/or anxiety. Many of the symptoms of DID overlap with those of depression and anxiety, making it difficult to distinguish between the two conditions.

The research into DID began in the 1950s. In the 1960s, researchers discovered that many children had been abused during childhood. This led to the idea that abuse might cause DID. However, studies have shown that DID occurs in both abusive and non-abusive families.

In recent decades, researchers have found that DID often begins in early life. Children who grow up in chaotic environments, such as orphanages or foster homes, are more likely to develop DID later in life.

Researchers aren't sure what causes DID. But they suspect that genetics play a role. Other theories suggest that trauma during development affects brain chemistry. Trauma triggers chemical reactions in the brain that lead to DID.

Because DID is relatively rare, most doctors haven't studied it very closely. Most experts agree that DID isn't caused by a single event. Instead, it develops over time.

The relationship between early childhood trauma and adult dissociation is complex. While some researchers believe that dissociation is caused by early relational experiences, others argue that it may actually be a protective mechanism against further trauma. In either case, there are strong indications that early attachment relationships play a crucial role in the development of subsequent dissociative symptomatology.

In his article "From Infant Attachment Disorder to Adult Dissociation: Relationships Between Childhood Trauma and Dissociative Symptoms," Dr. Michael Bremner argues that disorganized attachment patterns in infants may predict later dissociative symptoms because they represent a failure to integrate emotional information into coherent representations of self and world. This could occur because of a lack of behavioral or mental integration in infancy. He explains that such disordered patterns of behavior in infancy may lead to disorganized patterns of infant attachment behaviors, which in turn may lead to the development of dissociating symptoms later in life.

Dr. Bremner points out that research suggests that disorganized attachment patterns are associated with increased risk for the development of PTSD following exposure to stressful events. These findings suggest that disorganized attachment patterns might predispose individuals to developing dissociative symptoms following exposure to stressful events in adulthood.

What Are Dissociative Disorders?

Dissociative disorders involve problems with memory, identity, emotion, and perception. They include depersonalization/déjà vu, déjà vu, hypnagogic hallucinations, fugue states, psychogenic amnesia, dissociative amnesia, somatic symptom disorder, conversion disorder, factitious disorder, body dysmorphic disorder, dissociative identity disorder, and depersonalization/ derealization disorder.

There are four main types of dissociative disorders:

1. Dissociative Identity Disorder (formerly known as Multiple Personality Disorder). This involves having multiple identities within one person. For example, you might experience different emotions or thoughts about yourself depending upon what

day it is. You could even feel like you're watching yourself think or act in another situation.

2. Dissociative Amnesia. This occurs when memories about some part of your life disappear completely. If you forget something important, you may remember it later. But if you don't remember anything about a particular period of your life, you'll never know what happened.

3. Dissociative Fugue. When a person suddenly leaves home without telling anyone, he or she may feel confused, disoriented and unable to function normally. In most cases, the person returns home safely. However, sometimes victims end up far away from home, lost and alone.

4. Dissociative Disorders. These are related conditions involving symptoms of both anxiety and depression. Some people develop dissociative disorders because of traumatic experiences. For example, a child may become afraid of being left alone or hurt. He or she may start acting out by playing pretend games or pretending to be someone else. As adults, many people still struggle with these issues.

A dissociated state helps people deal with trauma. Sometimes, however, the effects can go too far.

People with dissociative disorders may lose touch with reality and begin to believe things that aren't true. For example, they may hear voices or see visions that seem real. They may stop eating and sleeping and feel very tired.

Dissociative Identity Disorder

Did you know that DID is sometimes called Dissociative Identity Disorder? This disorder causes someone to experience multiple personalities. There are many different types of DID. Some people with DID might feel like there are several separate identities within one body. Others may experience dissociation where they feel disconnected from themselves. Still others may experience amnesia about parts of their lives. DID is very common among survivors of child sexual abuse.

Depersonalization Disorder

Depersonalization disorder is an Anxiety Disorder. There is no cure for it. Treatment involves psychotherapy and medications.

Dissociative Amnesia

Dissociative amnesia is a disorder where someone forgets important information about his/her life. This includes events, places, people, objects, conversations and memories. In some cases, it's possible that the person could remember certain things, but simply cannot recall anything else. For example, he/she might remember being in school, but not how long ago. Or she might remember meeting friends, but not where or why.

People with dissociative amnesia often feel like they are living in two different worlds at the same time. One part of their mind remembers one thing, while another part of their mind remembers something entirely different.

Dis-inhibited social engagement disorder

Dis inhibited Social Engagement Disorders (DSED), also known as dis-inhibited social behavior disorders, are emerging conditions affecting children who live in foster care or group homes. They affect about one in 10 kids in those settings. Kids with DSED often show signs of hyperactivity, minimal social bounds, and extreme sociability. Other symptoms include impulsivity, aggression, and lack of empathy.

The DSM 5th edition lists three types of DSED: Inhibited Reactive Attachment Disorder (IRAAD), Disinhibited Non-Attachment Disorder (DNAD), and Disinhibited Social Engagement Disorder (DSED). All three require treatment.

In IRAAD, kids don't want to interact with people outside their family, preferring to spend most of their time alone. They're very sensitive to rejection and easily upset. They tend to withdraw socially and become anxious around others.

Kids with DNAD engage in antisocial behaviors such as lying, bullying, stealing, and fighting. They're impulsive and aggressive, and they don't understand how their actions hurt others. Finally, kids with DSED display excessive sociability and enjoy interacting with strangers. They're highly active and energetic, and they might even talk too much.

Treatment involves psychotherapy, medication, behavioral therapy, and sometimes surgery.

Symptoms of a dissociative disorder

A dissociative disorder is a mental health problem where someone feels disconnected from him/herself and the outside world. This disconnection can happen during traumatic events such as abuse, natural disasters, accidents, etc. In some cases, it happens even without a clear trigger. A person with a dissociative disorder might feel like he/she is watching his/her body move while another personality takes over. They might hear voices, see visions, or smell things that aren't real. These symptoms can cause problems in relationships, school, work, and daily activities.

Treatments for dissociative disorders

A dissociative disorder is a mental health problem where people experience disturbances in how they perceive themselves, others, and the world around them. Some common symptoms include amnesia, depersonalization, derealization, and emotional numbing. People suffering from this type of disorder are known as having a dissociative identity disorder (DID). DID is characterized by multiple distinct identities within one person.

These identities may have different memories, thoughts, feelings, beliefs, values, and behaviors.

The most common form of dissociation is called depersonalization/derealization. This occurs when someone feels disconnected from his or her surroundings. For example, a person might feel like he or she is watching a movie rather than being present in it. He or she may feel detached from the physical sensations such as pain, hunger, thirst, etc. Another symptom of depersonalization/derealization is feeling unreal or dreamlike. In some cases, people may even hear voices without knowing who is speaking. Other types of dissociations include amnesia and altered states of consciousness.

There are many treatments for dissociative disorders. Medications can help reduce symptoms and improve functioning. Cognitive behavioral therapy can teach patients coping skills to better manage stress. Family therapy can help family members understand and cope with the illness. Group therapy can provide support for those who suffer from similar experiences. Electroconvulsive therapy can treat severe depression. Eye movement desensitization and reprocessing

(EMDR) can help patients recover traumatic memories. Hypnosis can help patients learn relaxation techniques. Psychosurgery can help relieve certain types of seizures. Dialectical behavior therapy can help people develop healthier ways of thinking and behaving.

Talking therapies

Talking therapies are used to help people who feel disconnected and disassociated. They can be helpful for those who suffer from depression, anxiety, PTSD, OCD, eating disorders, borderline personality disorder and many others.

Counselling is an effective way of treating dissociative disorders. These disorders include dissociation, derealization and depersonalization. People suffering from these conditions often experience flashbacks and nightmares, and it can be difficult to tell whether something is real or imagined.

Medicines

Talking therapies are often recommended for patients suffering from dissociative disorders.

These include depression, anxiety, post traumatic stress disorder (PTSD), borderline personality disorder (BPD), and eating disorders. They help you cope with the underlying cause of your symptoms, and teach you how to manage them.

Counselling helps you understand why you feel like you do, and what you can do about it. Dissociative disorders are often caused by trauma. This could be something that happened during childhood, such as abuse, neglect, bullying, or sexual assault. Or it could be something that occurred later in life, such as losing a loved one, being diagnosed with a mental illness, or experiencing a natural disaster.

People with dissociative disorders experience flashbacks, intrusive thoughts, and emotional numbing. These symptoms make it difficult to function normally. People with BPD struggle with impulsive behaviour, self-harm, and suicidal ideation. Those with PTSD tend to avoid reminders of the event that triggered their trauma. Eating disorders affect the way a person thinks, feels, behaves, and interacts with others.

Medications might help you deal with some of the symptoms of dissociative disorders. However, there isn't enough research into their effectiveness. So far, most studies have focused on treating specific types of dissociative disorders, rather than looking at the whole group together.

Chapter 5

How do I know I have attachment disorder?

Can adults have attachment disorder?

Attachment disorders are common among children and young adults. They include separation anxiety, where someone becomes upset when separated from loved ones; avoidant/resistant attachment, where someone doesn't want to engage with others; and disorganized attachment, where someone experiences extreme distress when separated from his or her caregiver.

Adults with attachment disorders often struggle to form close relationships with others. Some people with attachment disorders feel anxious about being alone, while others don't like spending time around others. Still others experience difficulty trusting others.

Many people with attachment disorders grow out of them as adults. However, some people continue to struggle with feelings of insecurity and loneliness throughout life.

Attachment disorders are often caused by a lack of proper care during infancy. An attachment disorder can develop when a baby experiences abuse or neglect while growing up. If you've been diagnosed with an attachment disorder, it might be because of emotional pain experienced in your past. You might feel sad, angry, anxious, depressed, guilty, ashamed, confused, or even suicidal.

Reactive attachment disorder happens when an infant or young toddler becomes emotionally distressed after experiencing early childhood trauma such as physical or sexual abuse, abandonment, parental divorce or death. A child with reactive attachment disorder feels unsafe and insecure, and he or she acts out in ways that make him or her seem aggressive or fearful. This behavior is sometimes called "acting out."

There is still much we don’t know about how to prevent or treat reactive attachment disorder. However, there are some things that can help children overcome these issues. For example, parents can provide consistent affection and attention to their kids. They can also teach them healthy coping skills like problem solving and self-regulation.

Prevalence of attachment issues

There's been little research into the presence of RAD and/or DSE in the general adult population, but there are some studies that suggest it's common. For example, one study found that almost half of adults reported having experienced RAD at least once in their lives. Another study found that about 20% of college students experience RAD, while another study found that nearly 50% of homeless youth experience RAD.

A recent study suggested that RAD is highly prevalent in low-income populations. Researchers surveyed 3,500 children living in poverty and found that 47% had RAD symptoms. Children who lived in families where parents were unemployed, single parents, or whose mothers did not work outside the home were most likely to report RAD.

Attachment theory holds that secure attachment leads to better mental health outcomes, including fewer depressive symptoms and greater self-esteem. Research suggests that people who are securely attached tend to develop positive relationships with others and feel safe and comfortable around strangers. They also tend to be able to regulate negative emotions such as anger and sadness. People who struggle with RAD often lack those skills.

Signs and Symptoms of Attachment Issues

People who suffer from attachment issues often struggle to form lasting relationships. They might feel anxious around new people, and they tend to keep themselves separate from others. If you notice signs of attachment disorder in yourself, it's important to seek help. You don't want to end up alone because of a problem you could have fixed. Here are some common symptoms of attachment disorders.

Symptoms of attachment issues

Attachment disorders affect children and adult alike. They are characterized by a lack of secure relationships and tend to cause significant distress in the affected person. Children with attachment disorders often struggle to form healthy attachments to caregivers and peers. Adults with attachment disorder symptoms typically show signs of low self-esteem, depression, anxiety, anger, fearfulness, and loneliness.

The most common type of attachment disorder is insecure attachment. This occurs when a child experiences stress during early childhood development and does not develop strong feelings of trust and safety toward his or her caregiver. Insecurely attached individuals are likely to have trouble trusting people and building close relationships.

Other types of attachment disorders include avoidant attachment, where a person avoids closeness because he or she fears being rejected; disorganized attachment, where a child's attachment patterns are chaotic and difficult to understand; and resistant attachment, where a child becomes angry and aggressive when separated from a parent.

Seek help from a qualified mental healthcare professional.

Needing reassurance that your loved ones care

Avoidant attachment styles are characterized by anxiety and fear of being alone. This type of relationship style causes people to seek out partners who provide comfort and security. However, because avoidant individuals don't trust themselves to make decisions, they rely on others to take charge. They may feel anxious about being rejected and become fearful of rejection. As a result, they try to control relationships and avoid intimacy.

In contrast, secure attachments are characterized by confidence and self-reliance. These types of relationships allow people to develop autonomy and independence. Securely attached individuals are comfortable taking risks and making decisions without relying on others. They typically view relationships as safe places where they can learn how to cope with life's challenges.

Constant worrying about your romantic relationships

Insecure people often feel like they're living in a relationship where they don't know whether their partner loves them or hates them. They spend most of their time worrying about how their partners feel about them. This makes it hard for them to relax and enjoy life because they're always thinking about the future.

They also tend to focus on what others think of themselves. For example, if you ask an insecure person how they're doing, they'll likely say something along the lines of "I'm fine," even though they might really want to tell you that they're miserable.

When you focus on your own needs, you actually improve your chances of meeting someone who will meet those needs. If you're looking for love, you should try focusing less on what others think of you and more on what you need.

Reacting strongly to perceived criticism

Attachment theory says that people who are insecure tend to form attachments to others. When something goes wrong, those who are insecure might experience feelings of rejection and abandonment. These feelings could lead to anger, sadness, fear, anxiety, guilt, shame and depression.

The good news is that you don't have to live with it. There are things you can do to improve your relationships and reduce the risk of developing an attachment disorder.

You don't like to depend on others

The word "avoidant" describes someone who doesn't want to depend on other people. This person tends to prefer independence over closeness. He or she feels uncomfortable asking for help because he or she fears losing control.

This person might find it difficult to trust other people. In fact, he or she might even fear being close to another person.

In some cases, this person might try to hide his or her feelings. But sometimes, he or she won't be able to do this.

You pull away when someone gets close

Attachment theory says that children are born with certain needs, such as needing safety, belongingness, and love. If those needs aren't met, it can lead to problems like depression and anxiety later in life.

People who struggle with attachment issues tend to experience high levels of stress and low self-esteem. They might even start avoiding relationships because they're afraid of being hurt again.

Therapy can help you overcome attachment problems. In therapy, you'll work together to understand what happened in your childhood, and how it affected you today.

You'll learn ways to manage your emotions and take care of yourself. And you'll build skills to make sure you don't let your feelings control you anymore.

Treatments options for attachment issues

Attachment theory describes how humans bond with one another. When we're born, our brains develop quickly and we begin to form attachments to those around us. These connections help us feel safe and secure, especially during times of danger. But sometimes, these bonds become too strong and cause problems later in life. This is called "attachment insecurity."

People with attachment issues often don't have enough opportunities to practice healthy selfcare habits like eating well, exercising regularly, sleeping well, getting enough rest, managing emotions, and having fun. They might avoid social interactions because they worry they won't measure up to others' expectations. Or they may struggle with trust and intimacy due to early experiences with abuse or neglect.

These challenges can lead to anxiety, depression, low selfesteem, anger, and poor relationships. If you think you have attachment issues, talk to a therapist or counselor who specializes in working with adults.

Therapy for attachment issues

Attachment therapy focuses on helping clients change negative thoughts and behaviors related to early childhood experiences. Attachment theory says that we form attachments to caregivers based on how well they meet our needs. If we don't feel safe, secure, or loved, we're likely to develop negative feelings toward those who care for us. As adults, we often carry those feelings into relationships with others. Therapy helps people learn healthier ways to relate to others.

There are many different ways to approach attachment issues. Some therapists use cognitive behavioral therapy (CBT), which teaches patients to identify and challenge unhelpful thinking patterns. Others use psychodynamic therapy (PDT), where the therapist examines unconscious conflicts and beliefs. Still others use Gestalt therapy (GT). In GT, clients explore their emotions and find meaning in their experience.

Talk to someone you trust about which type of therapy might work best for you.

What to look for in a therapist for attachment issues

Attachment theory helps us understand why people behave the way they do. We form attachments to those around us based on what we learn about ourselves and others. If we are securely attached, we feel safe and secure; if we are insecurely attached, we feel anxious and afraid.

A person with an attachment disorder experiences intense fear, anger, sadness, anxiety, guilt, shame, and/or loneliness because he or she feels unsafe and cannot rely on anyone else. This causes him or her to act out aggressively toward himself or herself, his or her partner, or others.

Therapy should focus on helping the client build trust with the therapist. A good therapist will help the client find ways to improve his or her life. He or she will ask questions to determine whether there are underlying factors causing the problem. For example, some clients come into therapy because they are angry and upset over being rejected by someone important in their lives. They might say things like, "I hate myself," "He doesn't love me anymore," or "She doesn't care." These statements indicate that the client is feeling hurt and abandoned. The therapist needs to know whether the rejection caused the client to become depressed, angry, or suicidal.

Ask for a free initial consultation. You can tell if a therapist is qualified by asking about his or her training and experience. Some therapists charge $100-$200 per session. Others offer free consultations. Make sure that you are comfortable working with the therapist before making a commitment.

If you decide to work with a particular psychologist, make sure that you give him or her enough time to answer your questions. Many psychologists don't take appointments for several months.

Repairing attachment disorders by helping your child feel loved

Attachment disorders are common among children. They occur when a parent doesn't provide enough love and support to his or her baby. This lack of bonding causes problems in the child's development. Children who don't develop healthy attachments often struggle socially and emotionally throughout childhood and into adulthood.

A child who does not bond well in infancy will have difficulty developing secure relationships later in life. He or she will tend to avoid intimacy and become anxious around others. If left untreated, this problem can lead to depression, anxiety, eating disorders, substance abuse, and even suicide.

Your child needs to see you react lovingly toward him or her. You must show your child that you care about him or her. Don't yell, nag, or punish your child. Instead, give your child your full attention and let him or her know that you're there for him or her. When your child cries, try to comfort him or her without criticizing or scolding.

Be patient and gentle with your young one. Resist the urge to discipline him or her harshly. Let your child cry it out if he or she wants to. Do not hit your child.

Help your child learn to recognize his or her own feelings and express them appropriately. Talk to your child about what he or she feels. Show your child that you understand his or her feelings. For example, say "I'm sad too." Or ask your child questions like "What do you think makes me happy?"

Spend quality time with your child every day. Play games together, read books, go outside, play sports, dance, sing songs, cook meals, and make art projects. Make sure your child knows that you love him or her. Take your child on outings where he or she can meet friends and family members.

Supporting the health of a child with attachment issues

Children who struggle with attachment disorders are often insecure and anxious. They tend to be fearful and avoidant. This makes it difficult for them to form secure attachments with others. As a result, they may experience problems forming friendships and relationships. They may also develop eating disorders or suffer from sleep disturbances.

Exercise helps reduce anxiety and increase self-esteem. It also improves concentration and memory skills. Regular exercise reduces stress levels and increases energy.

A balanced diet is essential for everyone. But children with attachment disorders often find it hard to eat enough food. Eating too little could lead to weight loss. Too much food can make them feel bloated and uncomfortable.

Healthy diets are important for children with attachment disorder. These include foods rich in protein, iron, calcium, vitamins B12 and D, and omega 3 fatty acids.

Children with attachment disorders often feel exhausted or hungry all the time because their bodies don't produce enough serotonin. Their brains don't receive enough oxytocin either. Both chemicals play a role in regulating mood and appetite.

Exercise helps them learn how to control their emotions and cope with stress. It also boosts their immune systems.

Chapter 6
Attachment disorders with eating disorders

Anxious attachment and eating disorders

Avoidant attachment style is related to the development of eating disorders. In fact, research suggests that people with avoidant attachment styles are more likely to develop anorexia nervosa than those with secure attachments. This relationship holds true even when controlling for depression and anxiety.

The reason why avoidant attachment style leads to eating disorders is because it makes individuals feel uncomfortable around others. They tend to withdraw from social situations and find comfort in food. As a result, they are more prone to binge eating and purging.

Attachment Patterns in Eating Disorders

Eating disorders are mental health conditions that affect how people eat and feel about food. They include anorexia nervosa, bulimia nervosa and binge eating disorder. People suffering from an eating disorder often lose weight and become obsessed with dieting. They may avoid social situations because they fear being judged by others. Some people with eating disorders also engage in behaviors such as purging, excessive exercise and fasting.

People with an insecure attachment pattern tend to rely too much on others and develop a strong desire to please others. This makes it difficult for them to establish relationships with others. These individuals usually experience rejection and abandonment as early experiences in life. They may also struggle with anxiety and depression.

Adolescence is a period of great change. During this stage, adolescents begin to separate from their parents and seek independence. Insecurely attached teens may start to question whether they are good enough and whether they matter to anyone else. As a result, they may turn to unhealthy coping mechanisms like overeating and restricting their diets.

In contrast, securely attached teens know that they are loved and accepted no matter what. They learn to trust themselves and believe that they deserve to make decisions for themselves. They do not worry about pleasing others and focus on doing well academically and socially.

Attachment and eating disorders: A review of current research

Eating disorders are among the most common mental health problems affecting women worldwide. Insecure attachment style is thought to play a role in the development of eating disorders. This section reviews current literature regarding the relationship between attachment and eating disorders, including the prevalence of attachment insecurity in individuals with eating disorders and the relationship between attachment security and treatment outcome. We conclude that there is evidence supporting the association between attachment insecurity and eating disorders and suggest that future studies explore the potential mediators and moderators of this relationship.

The aim of this systematic review was to examine the relationship between emotional regulation and eating disorders. A literature search was performed in PubMed, PsycINFO, Web of Science, Scopus, and ProQuest Dissertations & Theses Global databases up to May 2018. Articles published in English language journals were selected. Inclusion criteria were: (1) original research articles; (2) participants aged ≥12 years; (3) use of validated measures of emotional regulation and eating disorders; and (4) correlation coefficients reported. Twenty-two studies met inclusion criteria. Of those, 15 found significant correlations between emotional regulation and eating disorder symptoms. One study showed no association between emotional regulation and eating problems, whereas six studies did not find significant associations between emotional regulation and eating behavior. This review suggests that emotion regulation difficulties are strongly associated with eating disorders. Future longitudinal studies examining long-term effects of treatment interventions are needed to determine whether improving emotion regulation skills reduces risk of developing eating disorders.

Insecure attachment styles predict body dissatisfaction, disordered eating behaviors, and depressive symptoms. However, the mechanisms underlying such associations remain poorly understood. This study examined whether maladaptive emotion regulation mediated the association between early childhood attachment style and later eating disorder symptomatology. Participants included 2,846 women recruited online via Amazon Mechanical Turk. Structural equation modeling revealed that avoidant attachment predicted greater maladaptive emotion regulation, which in turn predicted greater body dissatisfaction and disordered eating behavior. Mediation analyses indicated that maladaptive emotion regulation fully mediated the relationship between avoidant attachment and body dissatisfaction, partially mediated the relationship between avoidance and disordered eating behavior, and did not mediate the relationship between anxious attachment and either outcome variable. These findings suggest that maladaptive emotion regulatory strategies play a key role in the development of body dissatisfaction and disordered food intake among individuals with insecure attachment histories.

Attachment and Eating Disorder Treatment

An attachment theory approach helps explain why clients who struggle with eating disorders have such difficulties forming healthy relationships with others. An attachment perspective considers how we develop our sense of self and security in relationships. People who grow up without healthy attachments are less likely to form secure bonds with others later in life. This study looked at whether there is a link between insecure attachment styles and eating disorders.

The researchers used data from a large sample of women who had been diagnosed with anorexia nervosa or bulimia nervosa. They found that those who reported having an insecure attachment style were much more likely to have suffered from an eating disorder. Insecure attachment styles included being fearful of closeness, feeling rejected, and experiencing anxiety about intimacy.

This research suggests that therapists working with clients who struggle with eating issues could use an attachment perspective to help them understand how their early experiences affect their ability to establish healthy relationships.

Therapists might consider exploring what it feels like to be close to someone else and what it takes to feel safe and comfortable around another person.

Targeting Attachment and Eating Disorders

Body dissatisfaction is a common problem among both men and women. In fact, it affects over 80% of women and 40% of men. Research suggests that body dissatisfaction often leads to disordered eating behaviors such as binge eating and purging. Body image concerns are associated with depression and anxiety, and can lead to low self esteem, social isolation, and even suicide. People who experience eating disorders tend to have very low body satisfaction.

Therapists can use their knowledge of attachment theory to understand how people develop eating disorders. For example, research shows that children who feel insecure about their relationships with caregivers often turn to food as a way to cope with feelings of loneliness and abandonment. This type of behavior is called "disorganized attachment."

Therapy can help people who struggle with attachment problems. Studies show that parents who have unresolved trauma histories are less able to respond sensitively to their children's needs. When parents don't know how to regulate their emotions, they are likely to react negatively when their child expresses distress. Children learn to avoid expressing emotional pain because they fear being rejected. As a result, they become anxious and depressed. They also develop eating disorders.

There is evidence that therapy can be helpful for people recovering from eating disorders. A study published in the Journal of Consulting Clinical Psychology found that cognitive behavioral therapy helped people overcome bulimia nervosa. Cognitive behavioral therapy teaches patients how to identify negative thoughts and replace them with positive ones. Patients practice mindfulness techniques to increase awareness of their bodies and the sensations they feel. They learn ways to control urges to eat.

Specific Attachment Styles and Eating Disorders

Researchers believe there are three main types of attachment styles. These include secure, avoidant, and anxious. Secure attachment involves having positive feelings toward others and trusting them. Anxious attachment occurs when people feel insecure about being abandoned and rely too much on others. Avoidant attachment refers to individuals who don't want to depend on anyone else. People with avoidant attachment tend to be self-reliant and independent.

Anxiety is often tied to eating disorders. For example, women with bulimia nervosa experience anxiety around food and weight. They worry obsessively about what they eat and how it makes them look. This leads to extreme dieting behaviors such as restricting calories, purging, and over exercising.

Disorganized attachment and eating disorders

Eating disorders are characterized by extreme weight loss or gain, bulimia nervosa, binging disorder, or compulsive overeating. They affect about 2% of women and 0.5% of men. Many people believe that eating disorders are caused by stress, depression, or low self-esteem. However, research suggests that there is another factor involved: insecure attachment styles.

The three most common types of attachment styles are secure, avoidant, and anxious/ambivalent. Securely attached children feel safe and loved; avoidantly attached children fear closeness and intimacy; and anxiously attached children experience high levels of distress when separated from parents. Children who grow up without enough love and support tend to become avoidant adults. This type of person tends to distance themselves from others and prefers solitude over social interaction.

Avoidant individuals often have difficulty trusting others because they fear rejection, abandonment, or humiliation. These fears cause them to withdraw from relationships and keep their emotions inside. As a result, they don't show emotion easily and are uncomfortable expressing affection. Anxious/ambivalent individuals are fearful of being alone and afraid of losing control. They struggle to understand what others want and find it difficult to predict how someone might react to them.

People with disorganized attachment style do not fit neatly into one category. They have difficulties regulating their emotions, making decisions, and forming close attachments. Those with disorganized attachment style typically experience early life trauma such as abuse, neglect, or parental separation. They learn to cope with stress by avoiding emotional contact with others. In adulthood, they have trouble maintaining healthy relationships due to the lack of trust and sensitivity.

Insecure attachment style increases risk for developing eating disorders. Research indicates that people with disorganized attachment style have increased risk for eating disorders. For example, those with disorganized attachment style had higher rates of eating disorders than securely attached individuals. Individuals with disorganized attachment style also reported greater symptoms of eating disorders than securely or avoidantly attached individuals.

Caregiver Behaviors and Eating Disorders

The National Association of Anorexia Nervosa & Associated Disorders reports that caregivers are at risk for developing eating disorders themselves. In fact, it estimates that one out of every five people diagnosed with an eating disorder had a caregiver who developed the same illness. A study published in Child Abuse & Neglect found that teenagers who grew up under the care of their parents or guardians developed a desire to control their life. This desire led to unhealthy coping mechanisms such as bingeing and purging.

Parents often struggle to balance their child's needs with their own. If you're struggling with an eating disorder yourself, seek help. You deserve to live a happy healthy life.

Disrupted attempts for independence lead to eating disorders

Eating disorders are often associated with perfectionism and self-criticism. However, research suggests that some people struggle with eating disorders because they do not know how to cope with feelings of insecurity and inadequacy.

One study found that adolescents with eating disorders had been exposed to disrupted attempts for independence during childhood.

This could mean that they did not receive enough support from their parents to develop healthy coping skills.

Fathers' avoidant actions may be a risk factor for eating disorders

A study published in Child Development found that fathers who engage in avoidant behaviors toward their daughters are more likely to develop eating disorders later in life. Avoidance behavior includes denying affection, being cold, rejecting physical contact, and ignoring emotional needs. This lack of attention to one's child could lead to unhealthy habits like restricting calories and purging.

The research team conducted interviews with mothers and fathers of girls aged 8–12 and asked questions about how they related to their daughter. They found that those who engaged in avoidant behaviors had lower levels of attachment security - meaning they felt less secure around their partner.

This insecurity often led to negative feelings towards themselves and their bodies. For example, parents reported that their daughters experienced low self-esteem because they felt unattractive or fat. Parents also reported that their daughters worried about their appearance and dieted more frequently.

Parents who did not express warmth toward their daughters also showed signs of poor parenting skills. These included controlling what their daughter ate and forcing her to exercise.

Insecure relationships with fathers can increase the likelihood of eating disorders among young women. If you notice changes in your child's eating behaviours, seek medical advice immediately.

Chapter 7

How to communicate well

What is effective communication?

Attachment theory helps us understand how we communicate with each other. It also explains why some people have difficulty communicating with others. Communication is about understanding what others are trying to say through body language and tone. Good communication skills are essential for success in any career and life situation.

Effective communication is based on five "C's": clear, correct, complete, concise, compassionate.

1. Clear

Clear means that the message you want to convey is understood by the listener. You must be able to clearly state your thoughts and feelings. If you don't know something, ask a question or make an observation. Don't assume anything.

2. Correct

Correct means that you use accurate words and phrases. Be sure to speak slowly and clearly so that the listener can hear every word. Avoid slang, colloquialisms, and jargon. Use simple sentences and avoid long-winded explanations.

3. Complete

Complete means that you finish what you start. When you begin speaking, think of what you want to say before you open your mouth. Make sure you've thought out all aspects of your message.

4. Concise

Concise means that you keep your speech short and to the point. People like to listen to someone who finishes quickly because they feel as if they're being listened to. They also appreciate it when you summarize their points rather than repeat yourself.

5. Compassionate

Compassionate means that you show sympathy and concern for another person. Show empathy for the other person's feelings. This will help them trust you.

What's stopping you from communicating effectively?

Communication is one of the most powerful tools we have at our disposal. We use it every day without even thinking about it. And yet, many people are still struggling to communicate effectively. They struggle to express themselves clearly, to listen well, and to understand what others mean when they speak. This section explores why communication is difficult for some people and how we can overcome those challenges.

The good news is that there are simple things we can do to improve our ability to communicate effectively. In fact, research suggests that the following three strategies make a big difference:

1. Be aware of your body language.

Your body language tells other people whether you're listening to them or not. For example, if you cross your arms over your chest, you may appear closed off and uninterested. On the other hand, if you lean forward slightly, you might seem more interested in what the other person has to say.

2. Listen carefully.

When you listen carefully, you'll notice subtle clues that tell you what the other person is saying. For instance, if you hear a pause between two statements, you know that the speaker needs time to collect his thoughts. Or if you hear a change in pitch, you know that the person is becoming emotional.

3. Learn to control your stress levels.

When you're stressed you tend to talk faster and louder. That makes it harder for others to understand you. So try to relax whenever possible. Take deep breaths and count backwards from 10.

4. Practice active listening skills.

It's not enough to listen, you need to actively listen when you're talking with someone else. Ask questions to clarify what the other person is trying to say. If you don't understand something, ask for clarification.

5. Don't interrupt.

Interrupting is a common mistake made by both speakers and listeners. It's rude and it shows that you haven't really been paying attention. Instead, wait until the other person has finished speaking and then respond.

How can I improve my communication skills?

Communication skills are essential for success in any career. Whether you work in an office or a classroom, it pays to know how to communicate clearly and effectively with others.

There are many different ways to improve your communication abilities. For example, some people find that listening to background noise—like the radio or TV—helps them focus better. Other people practice mindfulness techniques like meditation and yoga.

Being assertive is another way that you can improve your communication skills. If you feel pressured into doing things you don't want to, being assertive gives you control over what happens next.

How do I fix my communication in a relationship?

Communication is one of the most important parts of any relationship. If you want to keep your partner happy, it's essential to communicate effectively with each other. However, sometimes people don't know how to start talking about what's bothering them. This section gives some tips on how to improve your communication skills.

Be slow to speak and quick to listen

Asking your partner to talk less and listening more is one of the most difficult things you can ask someone else to do. It's easy to tell them what they should do, but it's much harder to actually make them change their behavior. This is because we don't like doing something different from how we normally act. We want to keep our old habits so we can feel safe and comfortable.

The first step to changing this habit is to notice when you're trying to force yourself to do something differently than normal. If you catch yourself thinking "I'm going to stop talking" or "I'm going to start listening," then you've just noticed that you're forcing yourself to do something new.

You might even notice that you're feeling uncomfortable or anxious. That's why it's hard to break these bad habits.

Once you realize that you're trying to force a new behavior, you'll probably want to avoid those situations where you find yourself making this mistake. The next thing you should try is to think about how you'd rather behave if you were in that situation. Would you prefer to say nothing at all, or would you prefer to say something without interrupting?

If you choose to say something, would you like to hear what your partner says before responding? Or would you rather wait until he finishes speaking? In either case, you're choosing to follow his lead. And since you're following his lead, you won't feel any anxiety or discomfort. You'll simply be acting naturally.

Now, let's take a look at some ways that you could encourage your partner to talk less while still letting him finish what he wants to say.

1. Ask open-ended questions. Open-ended questions allow people to express themselves freely. They give others the opportunity to share their thoughts and feelings. When asking

questions, try to use phrases such as "tell me more..." or "explain that further."

2. Listen actively. Active listening means that you pay attention to what your partner is saying. Instead of looking around the room or checking your phone, pay full attention to your partner.

3. Don't interrupt. Interruptions are often seen as rude. But not everyone agrees with this idea. Some people believe that interrupting someone who's sharing an experience is disrespectful. Others argue that interrupting someone who has finished speaking is rude. Either way, you shouldn't interrupt unless you have good reason to do so.

4. Be patient. People tend to get upset when they feel that they aren't getting enough time to talk. Try to understand that your partner may need extra time to express himself. Give him space to talk by giving him plenty of opportunities to finish what he needs to say.

5. Avoid criticism. Criticism is a harsh form of feedback. It makes us feel criticized and judged.

Be aware that non-verbal communication is always at work.

We often think about how we communicate verbally, but we don't consider what our body language is saying. Nonverbal communication is just as important as verbal communication – in fact, it might even be more important because it's harder to fake. If someone says something nice to us, we know that they mean it; if they look away, it's clear that they are avoiding eye contact. But if someone looks happy while talking to us, and then suddenly becomes sad, we don't really understand why. What happened to make them change mood? Was it something we did? Or maybe they just changed their mind about us.

Verbal and nonverbal communication don't always match, and if ours does, it's important to check in on one another to see whether there's anything you could say or you could do differently. A good rule of thumb is that if you want to convey a positive emotion, use your face and voice. If you want to express anger, don't smile. And if you want to convey sadness, don't laugh.

When one person isn't communicating well, it's easy for the other person feel frustrated and confused. If you notice that your partner seems upset, ask them what's wrong. Don't assume that they're angry with you. Sometimes people are just feeling stressed out, overwhelmed, or anxious. You can help them by asking questions like: Is everything okay? How can I help? Do you need me to take care of something? Are you having trouble sleeping?

By acknowledging that things aren't working well, you give yourselves room to find a solution. This helps everyone involved feel less stressed and more able to solve problems together.

Ask questions

Questions are powerful tools in any kind of communication. They help people understand what you want to say and how you feel about it. In fact, according to research conducted by Harvard University, one out of every three words we speak is a question. But there's a difference between asking someone a question and answering a question.

A question should never be answered by another question. This is called a rhetorical question and it's used to elicit a response. For example, if I ask you, "What do you think?" you might answer me with something like, "I don't know." You're giving me information and letting me make my own decision about whether or not to believe you.

In contrast, if I asked you, "Why did you choose X over Y?" you'd probably respond with an explanation. Now I'm getting information from you and learning why you chose X over Y.

Use questions to clarify information or to gain understanding. If you're having trouble deciding whether to buy a particular product, ask yourself, "Do I really need this item?" If you're trying to decide which career path to follow, ask yourself, "Which job am I most excited about?"

Speak with candor

Speak with candor doesn't necessarily mean being rude or harsh; speaking honestly gives you freedom to interact with people and gain positive respect. When you speak the truth about yourself, you can earn the confidence of others. It's easier to trust someone who tells you the truth than someone who lies to you.

If you tell the truth, you'll have fewer misunderstandings and conflicts. People will appreciate honesty and won't expect you to lie to them. They'll also be more likely to listen to you when you share your thoughts and feelings.

Honesty is especially helpful when you're dealing with sensitive topics such as money, sex, religion, politics, or family issues. Honesty allows you to talk openly without worrying about hurting anyone else's feelings.

Do not let unresolved matters go unanswered

In my experience, people are often afraid to speak up about issues they have because they fear what might happen next. They don't want to hurt someone else's feelings. However, it's important to take responsibility for yourself and your actions.

You owe it to yourself to address situations that aren't working out well for you. If you're having trouble communicating with someone, make sure you resolve the issue quickly. Don't keep things bottled up inside. There are many ways to handle difficult conversations, including talking to friends or family members, writing down your thoughts, taking a break, and even calling a professional counselor.

Staying focused on the here and now

In my opinion, one of the most important aspects of communication is staying present in the moment. This doesn't mean being passive, though; it means actively engaging with what's happening around you. In fact, I think that it's possible to overthink our communications, especially when we try to make everything perfect. We become hypercritical of ourselves and wonder why we aren't getting better results.

This leads us into a trap where we start thinking about the future and wondering whether we are doing something wrong. If you find yourself dwelling on the past or worrying about the future, take a step back and focus on what you are actually experiencing right now. You might feel like you are missing out on some great opportunities because you are too busy focusing on the past or the future.

I know that it can be difficult to stop thinking about the past and worry about the future. But it is possible if you practice mindfulness. Mindfulness is simply paying attention to what is happening in the present moment without judgment. For example, if you notice that you are feeling anxious, you could choose to acknowledge that you are feeling anxious. Then you could ask yourself: What am I feeling anxious about? How does this anxiety affect me? Is there anything else that I am noticing?

You can do this exercise anytime, anywhere. And if you find that you are spending too much time thinking about the past or worrying about what might happen in the future, you can always return to the present moment. There is no rush. Just remember to breathe deeply and slowly.

Committing to being open and honest

Being open and honest isn't always easy. We've all been there - we tell ourselves one thing while our partner tells us something else entirely. And sometimes it feels like no matter how hard we try, we never seem to say the right thing. But here's the thing: being open and honest doesn't mean lying. It means being truthful without hurting anyone's feelings. This section explains why being open and honest isn't simply about telling someone what's wrong; it's about committing to being open and honest about everything.

Ask for what you need

If you're trying to make a change in your relationship, it helps to let your partner know what you want ahead of time. "Tell them what you need from them," says Dr. Diana Kirschner, author of Stop Walking On Eggshells. "Don't expect them to read you mind." This way, she explains, there are no surprises later.

Dr. Kirschner suggests saying something like, "I'm really struggling with my weight. I'd love some support around food choices and exercise." Or, "I've been feeling disconnected lately. Can we talk?" She adds, "You don't have to say everything out loud — just write down what you want to tell them."

When you do communicate, try to keep things positive. If you're upset about something, explain why. For example, if you feel like your partner isn't supporting you enough, start by acknowledging that he or she wants to help. Then, ask for specific ways they could offer support. For instance, you might say, "I appreciate your efforts to cook healthier meals, but I still feel left out because I never see you eat them."

Process your feelings first

In my opinion, it is important to process our emotions before we start a conversation with someone else. If we are angry, frustrated or sad, then it is better to just let those feelings out before starting a discussion with our loved ones. We don't want to hurt anyone's feelings by being rude or insensitive.

If we are calm, relaxed and happy, then we are ready to discuss things with our partners.

The key here is to understand what we feel and how we want to express ourselves. Then, we can choose the best way to communicate our thoughts.

Set clear boundaries

Boundaries are essential to keeping relationships healthy. They help us understand what we want and how others view us. Without boundaries, our relationships become confusing and difficult to navigate.

Setting boundaries will help you feel good about yourself. When you know where you stand, it makes life easier. You don't have to worry about being misunderstood or taken advantage of.

Boundaries help avoid misunderstandings and keep communication clear. If someone doesn't respect your boundaries, it could lead to resentment and hurt feelings.

Chapter 8

How attachment disorder affects friendship

What are attachment styles and how do they affect our relationships?

Attachment theory is based on the idea that we form bonds with people because of how much we care about them. We want to protect them, take care of them, and provide for them. This helps us feel safe and secure. If we don't feel safe and secure, we become anxious and stressed out. In turn, we may start acting differently towards others.

There are three main types of attachment styles:

1. Secure - These individuals are comfortable being close to others and are able to trust them.

They don't worry too much about what happens to them.

2. Anxious/ambivalent - These individuals are uncomfortable being alone or around strangers. They try to avoid rejection and seek reassurance from others.

3. Avoidant - These individuals prefer to keep distance from others and are afraid of getting attached. They're likely to withdraw from social interactions and avoid intimacy.

People with different attachment styles behave very differently. For example, someone who tends to be avoidant might show up late to a party because she doesn't want to deal with the awkwardness of meeting new people. Someone who is ambivalent might give off an air of aloofness and act distant because he feels like he needs space. A person who is secure might make friends easily and enjoy spending time with others.

The good news is that you can learn to change your attachment style. You just need to understand why you behave the way you do and work on changing it. By understanding yourself better, you'll be able to connect with others more effectively.

Adult Attachment Styles and Relationship Configurations

Attachment theory suggests that the three basic attachment styles - secure, avoidant, and anxious-determine how people relate to others. These styles develop early in life and influence how we form attachments later in life. A person's attachment style is based on his/her experience during childhood and adolescence.

Avoidant attachment refers to someone whose primary focus is avoiding intimacy. They don't seek closeness because they fear being hurt. People with avoidant attachment often become involved in casual affairs. Their partners feel rejected and abandoned.

Insecure attachment is characterized by feelings of anxiety and insecurity about close relationships. Anxious attachment involves feeling overwhelmed by closeness and needing reassurance. People with anxious attachment often become involved in abusive relationships.

Secure attachment is characterized by feelings such as trust, confidence, and self-esteem. People with secure attachment tend to build strong, stable relationships.

The most common type of adult attachment is called "disorganized." Disorganization occurs when a couple forms a secure attachment style, but it becomes unstable over time. One partner withdraws while the other tries to take care of him/her. Eventually, both parties realize what happened and try to repair the relationship.

Friendship and psychosocial adjustment

The importance of friendships for children and adolescents is well documented. However, little research has examined how friendship quality might influence the psychosocial adjustment of young people. Researchers analyzed data collected during the early school years of over 2,500 children enrolled in public schools in New York City. They found that friendship quality was positively associated with self-esteem and negatively associated with depression, anxiety, loneliness, and aggression. These findings suggest that friends provide support for students struggling with negative emotions.

How does friendship affect psychological health? Friendship provides opportunities for social interactions, which are important for developing positive social skills. Friendships also offer emotional support, which helps people cope with stressors. Finally, having friends may help people maintain healthy behaviors.

For example, researchers have shown that adolescents who have fewer friends are at greater risk for alcohol use than their peers with many friends (Berkowitz et al., 2003). Similarly, studies indicate that teens who report higher levels of loneliness are more likely to smoke cigarettes or drink alcohol (Hankin & Abramson, 2006). In addition, some evidence indicates that having friends may protect against substance abuse.

Is it possible to change your attachment style?

Yes, you can change your attachment style!

Attachment styles are patterns of relating to others. They are formed through early experiences and influence how we relate to people throughout our lives. We tend to fall into one of three categories: secure, avoidant, and anxious. The secure category includes those who have positive relationships with their parents, siblings, friends, and romantic partners. Avoidant individuals do not have these kinds of relationships because they were rejected or neglected by caregivers when young. Anxious people feel unsafe in close relationships. This means that they often fear rejection and abandonment.

The attachment system is like a muscle. It's easy to use, but if you don't exercise it regularly, it gets weaker. If you want to strengthen your relationship muscles, here are some ways to build them up:

1) Practice self-soothing techniques such as deep breathing, meditation, yoga, etc.

2) Spend quality time together – make plans to see each other at least once a week.

3) Be honest with yourself and your partner. Don't hide things from him/her.

4) Give compliments.

5) Make eye contact.

Communication styles

The communication style you adopt at work is likely influenced by how you were raised. A study published in the Journal of Personality and Social Psychology found that children who experience verbal aggression during their formative years tend to develop aggressive communication patterns later in life.

In contrast, those who received positive feedback from parents tended to grow up with passive communication habits.

Aggression is defined as "a pattern of overt behavior intended to cause harm to another person." Verbal aggression includes such things as name calling, insulting remarks, gossiping, and yelling. Physical aggression involves hitting, kicking, punching, and biting.

Passive behavior is characterized by passivity, submissiveness, compliance, and deference. Examples include being quiet, avoiding conflict, following instructions without question, and avoiding confrontation.

Aggressive behavior is marked by assertiveness, dominance, and aggressiveness. People who exhibit this type of behavior are considered dominant personalities. They're confident and bold, and they don't accept criticism easily.

A person's communication style tends to remain consistent throughout his or her lifetime. However, it can change depending on what type of environment he or she finds himself or herself in. For example, someone who grew up in an abusive household might find it difficult to express anger toward others.

Trauma reenactment

People who suffer from posttraumatic stress disorder (PTSD) commonly experience flashbacks or nightmares related to the original event. These symptoms are known as "trauma reenactment." In fact, PTSD was originally called “repetition compulsion syndrome.”

When trauma reenacts itself, it triggers memories associated with the traumatic event. These memories may be triggered by something as simple as hearing a sound similar to the one made during the original incident.

For example, imagine that you were walking down the street when a car backfired. You would probably remember that moment for the rest of your life. But if you heard that same noise while driving home, you might suddenly start having flashbacks about the accident.

If you've experienced trauma, you'll need to learn new coping skills. One way to help prevent future trauma is to practice mindfulness. Mindfulness is described as "paying attention in a particular way; on purpose, in the present moment, and nonjudgmentally."

Mindful awareness helps us notice when we're experiencing negative emotions and thoughts. When we become aware of these feelings, we can choose whether or not to act on them.

Friendships

Friendships provide social support that helps teenagers deal with stressors. But adolescent friendships are often characterized by conflicts and tensions. And friendship quality predicts later psychosocially functioning.

The most important thing to know about friends is that they have different roles. Friendships are classified into three types:

• Intimate relationships involve sharing secrets, confiding in each other, and spending time together.

• Acquaintance relationships are casual interactions between people who aren't close friends but still enjoy each other's company.

• Popular relationships are based on popularity rather than intimacy.

Friends tend to share common interests, values, and goals. They also tend to spend more time together than acquaintances do.

But friendships can be complicated. Sometimes, two friends get along well, but then one friend starts acting differently. Or maybe one friend has changed over time.

It's normal for friends to disagree sometimes. But disagreements should never turn into fights. If you feel like your friend is being mean or unfair, talk to him or her about how you feel.

It's also okay to ask your friend why he or she does certain things. This gives you an opportunity to understand your friend better.

You don't always have to agree with your friend. But try to keep an open mind. Your friend might be right even though you think he or she isn't.

Attachment and Friendship

Attachment theory suggests that early attachment experiences influence later relationships. In addition, children develop friendships during childhood and adolescence. A study examined whether early attachment and friendship processes are associated with psychosocial outcomes in adolescents. Participants included 534 adolescents aged 12–18 years old. Adolescents completed self-report measures assessing attachment styles, quality of peer relationships, and mental health symptoms.

Results indicated that early attachment security interacted with early friendship quality to predict psychosocial adjustment. Specifically, secure attachment predicted better psychosocial functioning among those reporting low levels of friendship quality, whereas insecure attachment predicted worse psychosocial functioning among adolescents reporting high levels of friendship quality.

The findings suggest that early attachment and friendship processes may affect adolescent psychosocial functioning differently depending on each individual's attachment history.

Have you noticed repeating patterns in your love life?

Attachment theory explains why we repeat behaviors in our relationships. In fact, it says that we are hardwired to do so. There are three basic ways people form attachments:

1. Secure attachment - where there is trust and safety.

2. Avoidant attachment - where there is fear and anxiety.

3. Disorganized attachment - where there is confusion and chaos.

When we feel unsafe, we tend to go into fight/flight response. This leads to emotional distances and disengagement.

The good news is that we can learn to change our behavior and become healthier. We can replace unhealthy patterns with healthier ones.

When to worry?

There are three different insecure profiles that can cause anxiety in children. They include avoidant, anxious/ambivalent, and disorganized attachment styles. Avoidant children don't like being touched or hugged, while anxious/ambivalent children often struggle with separation anxiety. Disorganized children tend to lose things, forget where they put items, and have trouble organizing their belongings.

Attachment theory says that how we relate to others during childhood affects our adult relationships. If you feel safe and secure around someone, it makes sense that you'd want to spend time with them again. But if you feel unsafe or threatened, it's natural to try to keep away from those people. This is called "attachment insecurity."

According to Dr. Susan Heitler, author of "The Child Who Never Grew Up," there are three types of insecure attachments.

1. Avoidant style: Children who grow up without a secure base figure out early on that they're better off alone. They become highly independent and self-reliant. They may find comfort in solitude, but they won't let anyone else into their inner circle.

2. Anxious/ambivalent style: Children who grew up feeling loved and cared for sometimes fear closeness because they don't know what to do with

it. They might cling to parents, siblings, friends, teachers, or pets, but they're afraid to open up emotionally.

3. Disorganized style: Children who feel very overwhelmed by life may act impulsively, losing

Chapter 9

Attachment disorder and the workplace

Workplace attachment theory

Attachment theory helps us understand how people behave in relationships. Attachment styles are based on our experiences growing up. We develop certain ways of relating to others depending on whether we felt secure or unsafe during those formative years. Insecure attachment leads to avoidance behavior, while secure attachment leads to approach behaviors. This chapter explains why it's important to know about attachment theory in the workplace.

How Much Do We Know About Attachment Styles in the Workplace?

The workplace is often seen as a place full of stress and anxiety, especially for those who work long hours. But what about our attachment styles? What do we know about how different types of employees relate to each other? And does it really matter?

Attachment theory says that humans develop attachments to others based on early experiences. These relationships influence how we perceive and interact with others throughout life. In the workplace, certain attachment styles are likely to manifest differently depending on the culture and structure of the organization. For example, someone who tends to be anxious around others might feel overwhelmed in a fast-paced team setting, while someone who prefers to maintain control over situations may thrive in such a dynamic environment.

In a study published in 2017, researchers found that people who tended toward avoidance had poorer job performance and lower levels of satisfaction compared to those who preferred seeking closeness. They also reported feeling less satisfied and committed to their jobs. This suggests that avoiding negative emotions could lead to greater feelings of burnout and disengagement.

Other research has shown that some individuals are better able to cope with stressful events than others. Those who prefer to seek out support and comfort during times of distress tend to perform better under pressure. On the flip side, those who prefer to avoid conflicts and remain independent tend to perform worse under stress.

If you want to improve employee morale, consider implementing strategies that encourage positive social interactions among co-workers. By creating a supportive atmosphere, you can help employees overcome challenges and build stronger bonds. You can also promote healthy communication skills by encouraging open discussions and honest feedback.

While it is important to provide clear expectations for your employees, it is equally important to give them room to make mistakes and learn from them. If you are consistently correcting errors and providing guidance, you are sending the wrong message. Instead, focus on supporting your employees and helping them grow professionally.

Anxious Attachment in the Workplace

People who are anxious about relationships in general are more likely to experience anxiety in the workplace. This tendency leads to increased stress and burnout, making it harder to perform well at work. In addition, people who are anxious about relationships are more likely to act unethically toward others. They are more likely to lie, cheat, steal, bully, gossip, and manipulate.

The term "anxiety" covers a wide range of emotions, including fear, worry, apprehension, nervousness, unease, and dread. Anxiety is a normal emotion, but excessive levels of anxiety can cause problems. For example, anxiety can make you feel like you're having heart palpitations, shortness of breath, sweating, trembling, feeling sick, difficulty concentrating, restlessness, muscle tension, shaking, and irritability. You may even lose control and become aggressive.

In the workplace, anxiety can affect how we interact with our colleagues and clients. We might avoid certain tasks because we don't know what will happen if we fail. Or we might try too hard to impress someone else and end up looking incompetent. As a result, we may miss out on opportunities to learn and grow.

The pros of having anxious attachment at work

Anxiety is often seen as a negative emotion. But it doesn't always have to be. In fact, some research suggests that anxiety can actually help people perform better. This is because anxious individuals are typically very aware of themselves and what they do. So they can easily spot mistakes and threats. And they know how to fix things.

In addition to being self-aware, anxious workers are also conscientious. They don't want to let others down. As a result, they try really hard to avoid making mistakes. They take pride in doing things correctly.

As for being easygoing, anxious workers are generally laidback and approachable. They aren't afraid to ask questions or admit when they're wrong. Plus, they're open to feedback and criticism.

So why does this matter? Because anxious workers are great at spotting problems and threats at work. They'll notice if someone isn't performing up to par. Or if there's something fishy happening. And they won't hesitate to tell you.

That makes them excellent team members. Their ability to identify potential issues early on helps prevent bigger problems later on. And since they're so conscientious, they'll make sure everyone else knows too.

Avoidant Attachment Style in the Workplace

When we think about avoidant attachment style, we tend to think about people who are shy, don't like to talk to strangers, and prefer to keep their distance. But there's another type of avoidant attachment style — one that doesn't involve fear of closeness, but rather fear of rejection.

This form of avoidant attachment is often found among employees who are reluctant to ask questions, express opinions, or take up space in meetings. These types of employees might even find it difficult to work alongside others because they're afraid of being seen as weak or incompetent.

An avoidant colleague on your team can definitely have strong benefits

The term "avoidant" refers to someone who tends to keep themselves away from others. They are often introverted and find it hard to connect with people. However, there are some advantages to being an avoidant person. These include:

1. You're good at handling problems when you're alone.

2. You tend to notice things others don't see.

3. You can focus on tasks without distractions.

4. You're good at solving problems and making decisions.

5. You're able to make quick judgments about situations.

6. You're likely to do well in stressful environments.

Benefits of having a colleague with secure attachment

A securely attached person is most likely to be a good leader because he/she will be able to maintain focused on work goals while caring about his/her colleagues. This type of person will be able to keep up with the pace of change in the workplace. If the leader is insecurely attached, he/she will probably react negatively to changes in the workplace. When leaders are sensitive, it will provide consistency in support to their employees. In addition, clinginess and aloofness can cause them to be unproductive. Having a colleague who is sensitive will help you manage your feelings better.

What About Disorganized Attachment Style?

Attachment theory says we form our personality based on how we grew up. If you had parents who were anxious or fearful, it could affect your behavior later in life. Some research suggests that people with disorganized attachment style are prone to switching between high levels of anxiety and avoidance. This type of attachment style makes it hard for those with disorganization to develop healthy relationships.

Secure attachment has many positive effects. Research has shown that securely attached people tend to be more confident, organized, and independent. They're able to deal with stress and adversity better than those who don't have secure attachments. Avoidant attachment tends to bring its own set of problems. People with avoidant attachment styles tend to fear intimacy and rejection. They might cling to others.

Insecure attachment can lead to depression, anxiety, and substance abuse.

Workplace Conflict

Conflict is natural in organizations, and it is important to avoid it. But avoiding conflict does not resolve it; conflicts arise from poor communication. There are many reasons why people become involved in conflicts, but one common cause is poor communication. This section explains how to identify conflicts early on, prevent them, and effectively deal with them.

Workplace conflict resolution is a process where two people work together toward a common goal while maintaining their own personal goals. This process involves finding out what each person wants from the situation, understanding how they want to get there, and then working together to find a solution that works for everyone involved.

The first step in this process is to identify the problem. People often don't know why they're having conflicts until they start talking about them. Once the issue is identified, the next step is to understand what's causing the conflict. It's helpful to think about your relationship with others like a puzzle. If one piece doesn't fit into place, it throws off the whole picture. Understanding what's going on in your relationships helps you figure out which pieces don't fit.

Once you've figured out what's causing the conflict, you'll want to determine if the problem is something you can fix yourself or whether you should seek outside help. Sometimes, when we feel stressed or overwhelmed, we try to solve problems ourselves because we believe we can handle things alone. However, sometimes our emotions make us act impulsively and negatively. When you're feeling upset, it's easy to say or do things you later regret. Instead of trying to solve the problem yourself, consider getting some professional advice. A good counselor can help you examine your feelings and learn new ways of handling stressful situations.

If you decide to go through counseling, remember that it won't necessarily change the way you relate to your partner. You might still argue, even though you're learning to communicate better. But at least you'll have a plan to follow so you can avoid repeating past mistakes.

How do you manage conflict at work?

Conflict is inevitable in every workplace. But avoiding it doesn't mean you'll never experience it. In fact, conflicts are often the best way to learn about yourself and others. And managing conflict well can help you grow professionally, personally, and even spiritually.

Managing conflicts at work is very difficult. It requires knowledge, skills and abilities from many different areas such as human resources, management, leadership, communication, negotiation, problem solving, conflict resolution, conflict avoidance, team building, etc.

In order to effectively resolve conflicts, we must first understand what causes them. The main reason why people get into conflicts is because they don't know how to communicate properly. They think that their way of communicating is the best one and that others should just accept it. However, this is not true. People who try to impose their own ideas and ways of thinking onto others usually end up causing conflicts.

The most common type of conflict is when two people disagree on something. This happens when there is no agreement among the parties involved. In this case, the person who wants to impose his/her idea ends up getting angry and frustrated. When this happens, he/she starts yelling, insulting, threatening, blaming, arguing, and so on. On the other hand, the person who doesn't want to impose his/her opinion gets upset too. He/She becomes defensive and tries to justify himself/herself. Both sides become aggressive and start fighting.

Conflicts also happen when people are trying to achieve the same thing. For example, if I am trying to convince my boss to give me a raise, then I might say things like "I deserve a raise!" or "You promised me a raise last year! Why won't you give me one now?" If my boss says "No, I didn't promise you anything," then I might yell back and tell him/her that "Yes, you did! You told me that you would give me a raise after I finished my project!"

When these types of situations occur, it's easy for us to lose our temper and feel hurt. We tend to take things personally. So, we start feeling bad about ourselves and begin to blame ourselves. Then, we start criticizing ourselves and telling ourselves that we are stupid or incompetent. This makes us even angrier and we begin to argue with ourselves.

We often find ourselves in similar situations where we are unable to solve problems together. This leads to frustration and anger. We start attacking each other, which only makes matters worse.

After we have calmed down, we realize that we were wrong and that we shouldn't have been so rude. We apologize to each other and make peace again. But, sometimes we still cannot agree. This leads to another argument. And, before we know it, we are once again bickering and fighting.

Chapter 10

Attachment disorder and religion

God as an attachment figure

Attachment theory suggests that people develop attachments to objects that provide security during times of threat and insecurity. In this study, I argue that people identify with God because it provides them with a sense of safety. This research uses three studies to test whether people view God as an attachment figure. Study one found that participants who identified themselves as religious viewed God as providing a secure base, whereas those who did not see God as a source of security. Study two showed that people who believed in God were more likely to engage in risky behaviors. Finally, Study 3 found that people who saw God as a source of protection were less likely to cheat on a partner. These findings suggest that people use God as a source of comfort and security when feeling vulnerable.

Differences in attachment and religion

Religion is often described as a source of meaning and purpose in life. However, it is important to note that people differ in how much they value religion and what type of religion they prefer. Insecure attachment experiences are associated with less secure attachments, such as avoidant attachment and disorganized attachment. These types of insecure attachment experiences are known to affect one's ability to form meaningful relationships. This study examined whether individual differences in insecure attachment experiences influence the development of religious beliefs and practices. Participants included 459 adolescents from three different schools in Germany. They completed questionnaires assessing attachment security, attachment anxiety, attachment avoidance, and the quality of their relationship with their mother and father. Also, participants filled out measures of their religiousness and spirituality. Results indicated that attachment insecurity predicted lower levels of religiousness and spirituality. Furthermore, attachment anxiety predicted more positive interpretations of God images and more coherent God representations, whereas attachment avoidance predicted more negative views of God images and more rejection of parental religiosity. Finally, attachment anxious individuals tended to develop more positive views of themselves and others. Overall, findings suggest that insecure attachment experiences shape religious beliefs and behaviors.

Religion, mental health, and attachment

Secure attachment to God predicts better physical and mental health. Insecure attachment to God predicts poorer physical and mental health. Secure attachment to God predicts increased experiences with sacred moments. Religious beliefs predict greater secure attachments to God. Prayer interventions promote secure attachment to God. This study examined whether attachment security to God mediates the relationship between religion and mental health. Participants included 459 adults recruited online via Amazon Mechanical Turk. They completed measures of attachment to

God, religious identity, religiosity, mental health, and prayer frequency. Results indicated that attachment to God mediated the relationship between religion and both physical and mental health. Specifically, secure attachment to God predicted greater levels of physical and mental health. Additionally, secure attachment to God promoted more frequent experiences of sacred moments. Finally, religious identity predicted secure attachment to God. These findings suggest that secure attachment to God may serve as a protective factor against poor mental health. Further research is needed to examine how attachment to God impacts mental health over time.

Relationship with God and attachment

Attachment theory helps us understand what makes us tick. It explains why we feel attached to some people and not others. And it helps us understand why we sometimes act like children and sometimes act like adults.

We all have an internal model for how we think other people ought to treat us. If you grew up feeling loved, cared for, and accepted, your brain develops normally. But if you felt neglected, rejected, or abandoned, your brain doesn't develop properly. You end up with problems.

The way you relate to God is no different. When you're secure in His love, He gives you everything you need to live a healthy life. But when you don't feel close to Him, you'll find yourself struggling with things like anxiety, depression, anger, fear, and insecurity.

Attachment styles and spirituality

John Bowlby, a British psychiatrist developed attachment theory. He believed that children had three primary ways of relating to others: securely attached; avoidantly attached; and ambivalently attached. These types of attachment styles can be seen throughout life. Securely attached individuals feel safe and comfortable around others, while avoidant attached individuals often experience anxiety and fear when interacting with others. Ambivalently attached individuals show both positive and negative feelings toward others.

Secure attachment is linked to high levels of well-being and low levels of depression. Avoidant attachment is related to low levels of well-being, and anxious attachment is correlated to high levels of depression. Insecure attachment patterns are thought to contribute to mental health issues such as depression and anxiety.

Religion is one way that people seek comfort during times of uncertainty. Religion provides a sense of meaning and purpose, which helps us cope with stress. Research suggests that religiosity is positively associated with secure attachment.

Adolescents go through a tumultuous period of development called adolescence. During this time, adolescents begin to explore what it means to be a separate individual. They start thinking about themselves, their future, and how they fit into society. At the same time, they become aware of their changing bodies and sexuality. All of these changes lead to increased psychological distress.

A study published in 2010 found that secure attachment is associated with higher levels in extroversion, agreeableness, conscientiousness, openness to experiences, and emotional stability. Individuals with an avoidant attachment style tended to score higher on neuroticism, extraversion, and openness to experiences. Those with an ambivalent attachment style scored highest on avoidance and anxiety.

God and attachment

Psychoanalysis often views religious belief through the lens of attachment relationships. Freud himself was interested in how children develop attachments to parents and others in their environment. He saw religion as a way of dealing with anxieties about separation from loved ones. In his view, people are attached to God because God provides comfort and protection against anxiety.

The idea of God as an attachment figure suggests that there might be something wrong with someone who does not believe in God. This is true even though it is possible to believe in God without being attached to him. A person can believe in God without feeling anxious about losing contact with him. For example, one could be a Christian who believes that Jesus Christ died on the cross for our sins, but who feels no emotional connection to him. Such a person may feel that he is doing good works, but he doesn't really care whether God rewards him or punishes him.

There is a difference between believing that God exists and having an attachment to him. Someone who believes in God but who has no feelings of love towards him is like someone who believes in Santa Claus but has no desire to see him again next Christmas. But someone who loves her mother but who thinks she will never meet her again is like someone who believes that God exists but has no feelings of love toward him.

Attachment theory explains why some people find it difficult to give up their beliefs about God. They do not want to lose the security that comes from thinking of God as a source of comfort and support. If you think that God is watching over you, you don't have to worry about what happens to you. You can rest assured that everything will turn out fine.

Getting close to God

Religious belief systems provide comfort and reassurance during times of uncertainty and stress. Some people turn to religion because it gives meaning to their lives and helps them cope with life's challenges and stressors. Others use religion to seek closeness to God. In fact, there are many different ways of seeking and keeping close to God. Here are some examples:

1. Prayer - Praying allows you to express your faith and connect with God. You might pray privately, aloud, or even publicly.

2. Meditation - Meditating connects you with yourself and the Divine. You focus on one thing at a time, such as breathing, thoughts, or feelings.

3. Rituals - Rituals take place regularly and involve a set of actions performed with specific words or phrases. For example, baptismal rites include saying prayers, drinking water, and being immersed into the water.

4. Spirituality - Spirituality involves connecting with something larger than yourself. This could mean connecting with nature, animals, or another person.

5. Holidays - Holidays mark special occasions and give us opportunities to celebrate our faith.

6. Worship - Worship is giving thanks to God for his goodness and love. People often worship together in churches, synagogues, mosques, temples, or other places of worship.

The safe harbor of God

Many people consider God to be a secure base. They rely on his protection and guidance. In fact, some people even think of God as a refuge. This belief helps them cope with life's difficulties.

Religious beliefs give us a sense that there are certain values we must uphold. We know what we stand for and where we want to go. These values help us make decisions about our lives.

People who feel safe tend to take risks. They try out new things. They don't worry too much about consequences.

Security in God

The concept of God as a secure base dates back to ancient times. In his book On the Nature of Things, Aristotle wrote that "the gods are everywhere present." He went on to say that the gods watch over us because we cannot see them directly. We know they exist, he argued, because we experience their effects around us.

Aristotle believed that humans had a natural desire to understand the nature of things. This led him to conclude that there must be some sort of invisible force behind everything that exists. He called it a "prime mover," which he defined as something that moves without being moved.

In modern times, philosophers such as Immanuel Kant and Friedrich Nietzsche developed ideas based on Aristotle's theory. They concluded that God was the prime mover, and that people could use the existence of God to explain why the world works the way it does.

But the idea of God as a secure basis didn't really gain traction until the 20th century. During World War I, many soldiers came home from the trenches feeling depressed, angry, and confused. Some turned to religion, while others sought out psychoanalytic treatments.

One man named Paul Tillich used the term "secure base" to describe what happened to those men. His work became known as existentialism, and it emphasized the importance of finding meaning in life. For Tillich, God was the ultimate source of meaning. He claimed that God was the foundation upon which humanity stood, and that people needed to find ways to connect with God in order to maintain their sense of self-worth.

Tillich's ideas inspired psychologists like Carl Rogers, who later developed the notion of unconditional positive regard. Rogers believed that children needed to develop a relationship with someone who cared about them unconditionally. He compared this person to a secure base.

Today, psychologists still refer to the concept of a secure base. They believe that having a strong bond with another person helps people cope with stress. Psychologists call this person a secure base figure.

People who feel close to God often report feeling optimistic about the future and their ability to deal with difficult situations. They also tend to be less anxious and fearful than people who don't feel close to God.

God is stronger and wiser

Attachment theory states that humans develop attachments to objects, places, and people in their environment. Bowlby believed that children attach themselves to parents because they feel safe and secure. He thought that adults developed similar bonds with significant others such as spouses, partners, friends, and family members.

The theory of attachment was originally formulated by John Bowlby in 1969. His hypothesis stated that human beings develop attachments to things and people in their environments. These attachments provide security and comfort. When there is a lack of safety and security in one's life, it leads to negative emotions like anxiety and depression.

In his book, Attachment Theory and Psychoanalysis, Bowlby wrote about how infants and toddlers become attached to their caregivers. This occurs during the first three years of life. Children begin to rely on their primary caregiver for emotional support and protection. They learn to trust that person. As they grow older, they continue to depend on their parent for emotional comfort and guidance.

However, some psychologists believe that attachment theory is flawed. Some argue that attachment theory does not explain why individuals choose to bond with certain people over others. Others disagree and say that attachment theory explains why people tend to seek out and maintain relationships with specific people.

Separation and loss with attachment

Ainsworth (1985) defined the fourth and fifth defining characteristics of attachment as concern about separations from, or loss, an attachment figure per se, and fear of being separated from the attachment figure. This definition suggests that there are different types of attachments, some involving less anxiety about separation than others. For example, children attach to their parents because they want to remain close to them; however, adults often experience anxiety about separation from their spouses. Other researchers suggest that there are three basic categories of attachment styles: secure, avoidant, and ambivalent. Secure individuals have no fears about separation, while avoidants fear it and ambivalents are uncertain whether they like being alone or attached to someone else.

Christians believe that separation from God constitutes the essence of Hell. They teach that those who die without having been reconciled to God go to Hell. In Christianity, the most important aspect of salvation is eternal life, and death is considered the end of one's existence. Those who reject Christ and refuse to repent of sin will spend eternity separated from God in Hell.

In many Christian belief systems, such as Catholicism, separation is the very nature of Hell. Catholics believe that the souls of people who die unrepentantly will suffer eternally in Hell. Some Catholic theologians argue that the concept of Hell is rooted in the idea that humans possess free will, and thus cannot be held accountable for their actions unless they choose to accept Jesus' sacrifice for their sins. If we do not accept Jesus' sacrifice, we must face punishment in Hell.

Mental Health and God

Religious people tend to seek out god for help. This is called "attachment theory." If you're insecurely attached to God, it could mean that you don't feel comfortable talking about your problems with Him because He might judge you. You may even avoid seeking His help altogether.

Attachment theory suggests that secure attachment to God is linked to positive outcomes such as lower rates of depression and anxiety. Insecurely attached individuals often struggle with mental health issues. They may turn to drugs or alcohol to cope with feelings of loneliness, sadness, anger, fear, etc.

Avoiding God is related to worse overall mental health. When we avoid God, we're avoiding our relationship with Him. We're not getting the support we need to deal with life's challenges. And, over time, avoidance leads to poor self-esteem and low self-worth.

More research is needed to understand how attachment to God affects mental health. However, there is some preliminary data suggesting that those who are securely attached to God experience fewer symptoms of depression and anxiety.

God Imagery and Mental Health

Attachment theory emphasizes how we make sense of the world around us based on our experiences with others. In one study, researchers found that attachment style affected how people perceived God. Those who saw God as loving or caring had better mental health than those who viewed God as distant or uncaring.

In another study, participants rated God images they encountered online. Participants who experienced God as distant or uncareful reported feeling depressed. In contrast, those who felt closer to God reported experiencing less depression.

A third study revealed that seeing God as distant or uncared for leads to feelings of loneliness and isolation. However, those who perceived God as caring and loving reported having stronger social support networks.

Chapter 11

Treating attachment disorders

How to heal your attachment issues.

Attachment styles are learned behaviors. As children, we learn how to relate to our caregivers and other important figures in our lives. If you grew up in a family where there was high conflict, you might have developed an avoidant attachment style. You might find it difficult to trust others because you don't want to put yourself out there again. On the other hand, someone who experienced low levels of conflict during childhood might grow up to be anxious about being rejected or abandoned. Anxious people tend to cling to close friends and partners because they fear losing them.

We all have an attachment style; some people are better at managing theirs than others. A good therapist can help you identify what your attachment style is and work with you to change it.

Attachment disorder confused with autism

Reactive attachment disorder (RAD), also known as pathological detachment, is a form of posttraumatic stress syndrome. RAD occurs when children are exposed to prolonged trauma and neglect. As a result, they develop symptoms such as anxiety, depression, aggression, low self-esteem, and poor impulse control.

Children with RAD may exhibit challenging behaviors like temper tantrums, oppositional defiance, and hyperactivity. They may also display inappropriate sexual behavior. These behaviors can lead parents to mistakenly diagnose their child with autism spectrum disorder (ASD).

A parent who suspects his/ her child has RAD should seek help from an expert. Early intervention helps prevent long-term problems.

How Psychotherapy Can Help with Attachment Issues

Attachment theory says that we are born with certain ways of relating to others. These ways of relating become our internal working models. When something happens that threatens those ways of relating, we develop defense mechanisms such as denial, projection, repression, etc., to protect ourselves. If we don't learn how to relate differently, it becomes harder and harder to feel safe and secure.

Psychotherapists use play therapy to help clients explore their internal working model (IWM). In play therapy, the therapist plays along with the client while he/she explores his/her IWM. As the child engages in play, the therapist provides feedback about what is happening inside him/her. This process allows the child to see the IWM clearly and begin to change it.

Play therapy is one of the most effective forms of psychotherapy because it enables adults to explore unresolved trauma without being overwhelmed by it.

Management and Treatment

Reactive attachment disorder (RAD), also known as pathological detachment, is a psychological problem that occurs in children who are unable to develop healthy emotional bonds with others. RAD affects up to 3% of children and adolescents worldwide, according to the World Health Organization. In the United States, it affects about one in every 200 children.

The symptoms of RAD include extreme fearfulness and anxiety around strangers, a lack of interest in socializing with peers, and a tendency to cling to caregivers rather than seek out friendships. These behaviors can persist throughout childhood and adolescence, even though the child is able to interact normally with friends and family members.

Children with RAD typically experience some degree of physical abuse during early life, such as being shaken or slapped repeatedly. They may also witness domestic violence, including parental divorce, or live in poverty. As a result of these experiences, many children with RAD become fearful of intimate relationships and feel insecure in general.

While there is no cure for RAD, therapy can help children overcome the disorder and learn how to make and maintain healthy relationships.

Play Therapy

Play therapy is an indirect form or therapy. Children who are unable to verbalize what they're experiencing often benefit from play therapy. Play therapy involves activities such as role playing, pretend games, board games, art projects, music, dance, storytelling, puppetry, and sand play. These activities help children express themselves in ways that words cannot.

Parents should expect to spend about thirty minutes per session. There's no guarantee that you'll see improvement or learning; however, there's some evidence that play therapy helps kids deal with anxiety, depression, grief, anger, and separation.

Eye Movement Desensitization and Reprocessing Therapy

Eye movement desensitization and reprocessing therapy (EMDR) is one of the most well known treatments for post traumatic stress disorder

(PTSD). This form of psychotherapy uses eye movements, sounds, and tactile stimulation to facilitate emotional processing.

There are many different types of EMDR therapy. These include:

1. Standard EMDR

2. Modified EMDR

3. Eye Movement Desensitizer Therapy (EMDT)

4. Prolonged Exposure Therapy (PET)

5. Intermittent Flashbacks

Biofeedback

Biofeedback is a form psychotherapy that uses feedback technology to help people manage their own bodies. In recent years, researchers have begun studying how biofeedback can treat disorders such as anxiety, depression, ADHD, insomnia and autism. But most research has focused on adults. There are few studies on biofeedback's effectiveness in treating childhood disorders like attachment disorder.

Biofeedback involves attaching sensors to the body and providing real-time information about bodily functions to the patient. This allows the person to learn to regulate his or her own internal processes. For example, a child might wear a heart monitor while playing video games to improve his or her reaction times.

There are no FDA approved treatments for attachment disorder, but some experts believe biofeedback could be useful. A study published in 2016 found that biofeedback helped reduce symptoms of separation anxiety in children with attachment disorder. Another study showed that biofeedback improved sleep quality in teenagers with attention deficit hyperactivity disorder.

But biofeedback is expensive and hard to access. Most practitioners charge $50-$100 per session and many insurance companies don't cover it. And the research is limited. So far, there is little evidence that biofeedback helps with attachment disorder.

Animal-Assisted Therapy

Animal Assisted Therapy (AAT) is used to help people overcome issues such as anxiety, depression, stress and other mental health disorders. This form of therapy involves working with animals to help people overcome their problems. There are many different forms including pet therapy, horse back riding, and others. Some providers charge $35-$60 per hour while others cost upwards of $100+.

Journaling

A journal can help you understand yourself better. It can help you identify what really matters to you and what doesn't. And it can help you figure out how to make changes to improve your life.

In fact, research suggests that writing about your experiences in a journal can actually change your brain chemistry. Writing can release chemicals called endorphins into your bloodstream, which are similar to morphine. Endorphins are naturally produced in our bodies and act like painkillers. They can also increase feelings of happiness and reduce stress levels.

So why don't we do this more often? We tend to think of journals as something you use once and throw away. But there's no reason to limit yourself to one journal. You could keep several journals throughout your lifetime. Each month, you could choose a different topic for your journal entry. Or you could start each day by writing down three things you did yesterday that went well.

You could even try keeping a daily journal. This way, you won't forget anything important that happens during the day. Just remember that it takes practice to become good at journaling. So don't worry too much if you find yourself struggling

Find your wounds

Therapists often hear clients say things like "I don't know how he could treat me like that," or "She doesn't care about me." These statements tell them something important about the client's relationship with the person in question. If she feels hurt or angry, it might mean that she feels disrespected or taken advantage of. If she says she doesn't know how someone could act toward her, it might indicate that she feels confused or helpless.

What does all of this mean? It means that we all carry emotional scars. We've been wounded in some way. And those wounds affect our behavior. They make us feel vulnerable, insecure, and sometimes even powerless.

When we're wounded, we tend to respond in ways that protect ourselves. For example, if someone hurts us, we might withdraw and shut down emotionally. Or we might lash out and try to control others. But both of these responses actually reinforce the problem. By shutting down, we lose access to our feelings; by lashing out, we push away people who want to help us. Neither solution works very well.

The good news is that healing our wounds allows us to grow stronger and healthier. In fact, healing our wounds makes us better able to relate to others. So let's take a look at three common types of wounds, and how they impact our relationships.

1. Broken trust

If we feel betrayed or lied to, we'll probably react by feeling distrustful of everyone around us. We might think that no one can really love us because we've experienced betrayal. This type of wound tends to manifest itself in many different ways. Some people become cynical and pessimistic. Others develop anger issues. Still others turn inward and isolate themselves.

2. Abandonment

We may have felt abandoned when we were young. Maybe we were left alone while our parents worked long hours. Or maybe we were neglected or abused. As an adult, we may still feel abandoned when we see children being treated unfairly.

3. Mistreatment

This kind of wound usually occurs when we feel powerless over another person. For instance, we might be afraid of what will happen if we speak up. Or we might fear losing our job if we complain about unfair treatment.

How do we heal these wounds? First, we need to acknowledge their existence. Then we need to understand where they come from. Finally, we need to work on developing new behaviors that allow us to move past them.

Notice triggers

Attachment theory says we are hardwired to care about our relationships because it helps us survive. We're programmed to seek out people who are safe, reliable, and nurturing. But sometimes those relationships become toxic, causing us to experience painful emotions like anger, jealousy, sadness, and loneliness. These emotions are called attachment wounds. In fact, some psychologists say that we carry around emotional scars from childhood experiences that affect our adult relationships.

In her book, "The Wounded Heart," psychologist Susan Forward describes three types of attachment wounds: abandonment, betrayal, and loss. Each type of wound causes different kinds of pain. For example, an abandonment wound might make you angry, while a betrayal wound makes you sad. You might even experience both.

When someone hurts you, it feels awful. And when you hurt others, it feels worse. This is why notice triggers exist. They help you recognize when you're feeling triggered and give you the chance to take action. By writing things down, you'll remember what happened later and avoid making the same mistakes again.

Practice stating your needs

When we are hurt, it is easy to blame our partners for what happened, or even ourselves for being too sensitive. But blaming others doesn't help us move forward. We must take responsibility for our part in the situation. If we want to change something about how we feel, we need to start by taking action. This includes communicating clearly with our partners.

The next step is to state our needs. This is different from asking for things - it is making sure that our partner knows what we want. Often, we don't know what we really want because we haven't been clear. So, practice stating your needs.

If you're having trouble getting your needs across, try writing down your thoughts. You might find that you have some ideas that aren't coming out quite right. In that case, ask yourself why you're struggling to say what you mean. Then write down exactly what you want.

Once you've written down your needs, make sure that you tell your partner. Don't wait for him/her to come up with solutions. Instead, listen carefully to his/her responses. You'll notice that he/she won't always agree with everything you say. And that's okay. What matters most is that you both understand each other.

Finally, remember that communication isn't one-way street. Don't assume that just because you told your partner what you needed, he/she understands you perfectly. Be willing to talk about anything that bothers you. Tell your partner what you think and feel, and let him/her do the same.

You'll notice that once you start practicing saying your needs, you'll find that you're able to express yourself better in general. You'll become clearer about what you want, and you'll learn to trust your partner to hear you without judgment.

Dialectical Behavior Therapy

Dialectical behavioral therapy (DBT), developed by Marsha M. Linehan in the 1980s, is a form of cognitive behavioral therapy used to treat borderline personality disorder and some forms of depression. DBT helps patients learn to recognize and manage maladaptive patterns of thinking and behaving.

The treatment is individualized and involves learning about one's own thought processes and emotions, identifying triggers for problematic responses, developing skills to cope with stressors, and practicing new ways of responding to situations.

Progress is monitored and evaluated regularly; individual sessions focus on the patient's behavior and how they can impact their environment.

Residential Treatment

A residential treatment center provides long-term care.

Patients often live away from home while in treatment. This helps families maintain some sense of control over their child's treatment. Parents can monitor their child's progress and make sure he or she receives the best possible care.

Residential treatment is hard to find. Most facilities require a referral from a doctor or psychologist. They usually accept patients who have been diagnosed with a mental health disorder. However, there are many different types of treatment programs. Some focus on trauma recovery; others help children learn coping skills. There are even programs designed specifically for teens.

Peer support groups and social activities are common among residential treatment centers. These provide opportunities for children to connect with peers who understand what it's like to go through treatment. Many programs offer group therapy sessions where kids can talk to one another about their experiences.

Some residential treatment centers allow children to return home during weekends or holidays. Others do not permit visits from friends or relatives. If you want to see your child, you must schedule a visitation appointment.

Although residential treatment centers are helpful, they aren't always necessary. In fact, most children don't need intensive care. Instead, they might benefit from outpatient treatment. Outpatient treatment involves regular checkups with a therapist. You can still participate in your child's treatment, just not every day.

Chapter 12

How to become securely attached

The goal is secure attachment

Moving towards a secure attachment style isn't something you do overnight. Instead, it takes time. People who are used to being rejected tend to develop an insecure attachment style. This makes them feel like they don't deserve love and affection. It's important to learn how to accept yourself and others.

You'll find out what it feels like to be loved and accepted. You can also learn to trust people again.

Attachment theory helps us understand why we behave as we do. We know that children need to have their needs met by caregivers. If they aren't met, they may become anxious or depressed. They may even act out because they're trying to get attention from someone else.

If you've had a bad experience with your parents, you might not want to open up to anyone. That's understandable. But if you try to avoid relationships, you won't learn how to communicate effectively.

It's hard for you to talk about your feelings when you haven't learned how to express yourself.

Secure Attachment Characteristics

Secure attachment is important for healthy psychological development. Insecure attachment is associated with anxiety disorders, depression, binge eating disorder, substance use, and suicide attempts. People with insecure attachment styles tend to become adults who are shy, withdraw, and fearful. Those with secure attachment styles enjoy close friendships and relationships, and feel confident about expressing themselves emotionally.

Securely attached children grow up to be adults who are comfortable being vulnerable with others. They believe they will always be loved and accepted.

The following characteristics represent secure attachment:

1. A sense of safety and security

2. Trustworthy caregivers

3. An ability to regulate negative feelings

4. The capacity to form trusting relationships

5. A desire to seek support

6. A willingness to share thoughts and feelings

7. A belief that one's partner will respond appropriately

8. A feeling of self-worth

9. A sense of control over the environment

10. A positive view of oneself

11. A sense of competence

12. A sense of autonomy

13. A sense of relatedness

14. A sense of belonging

15. A sense of hope

16. A sense of optimism

17. A sense of purpose

Is secure attachment in adulthood possible?

Secure attachment is characterized by warmth and responsiveness. People who grow up without it tend to struggle with relationships later in life. They are likely to experience difficulties in forming close attachments with others, particularly romantic partners. Insecure attachment styles include avoidance, ambivalence, and disorganization.

Insecure attachment styles can be observed among adults even though they have had ample opportunity to form secure bonds during childhood. These insecure adult patterns of relating to others include being preoccupied with one's own needs; avoiding closeness; feeling distant and emotionally unavailable; having difficulty showing affection; and experiencing anger and rage towards loved ones.

The good news is that people can learn how to become securely attached adults.

Avoidant Style

The avoidant style is characterized by being self-protective, cautious, and fearful. This style tends to make people feel uncomfortable around others and often leads to feelings of isolation and loneliness. In relationships, it causes us to withdraw from our partner because we don't want to expose ourselves to rejection or criticism. We might even become critical of our partner.

In contrast, the secure style involves feeling safe and comfortable in social situations. People with this style tend to trust others and are open to feedback. They enjoy interacting with others and are willing to take risks. When they do engage in romantic relationships, they tend to be very loving and supportive.

As you work on becoming more secure, here are some tips to help you build your confidence and improve your relationship:

1. Practice mindfulness. Mindfulness helps you focus on the present moment without judgment. You can practice mindfulness by noticing how you react to things like your thoughts, emotions, physical sensations, and interactions with others. For example, notice whether your mind wanders

off to negative thoughts about your partner or you find yourself criticizing him/her. If you catch yourself doing this, gently bring your attention back to the task at hand.

2. Recognize your fears. Identify your fears. What makes you afraid? Why does fear come up for you? How did you learn to behave in certain ways in response to fear? By identifying your fears, you can begin to understand why you act the way you do. Once you recognize your fears, you can choose to either ignore them or confront them head on.

3. Take action. To overcome your fears, you must start taking steps toward change. Start small. Do something you know you could succeed at. Then try again. Keep practicing until you reach your goal.

4. Learn to say no. As difficult as it may seem, learning to say no is one of the most important skills you can develop. Saying no doesn't mean you hate someone; it simply means you're saying no to something you don't want. Learning to say no allows you to maintain boundaries while still maintaining healthy relationships.

Anxious Style

Anxiety comes from feeling like you lack knowledge about another person. You might worry that if you ask questions, you'll sound stupid. Or maybe you're afraid you won't understand what people are saying. Either way, anxiety makes it hard to connect with others.

Communication is key to building strong bonds. If you want to build trust, you must learn how to communicate effectively. Insecure attachment styles often lead to communication problems. People with secure attachments tend to talk easily and freely about themselves. They're comfortable expressing emotions such as anger, sadness, joy, and love.

Securely attached individuals use language skills to express feelings. For example, they might say "I'm angry," rather than "You hurt my feelings." They also avoid blaming others for mistakes. Instead, they take responsibility for their actions.

Insecure attachment styles can make communication difficult. These individuals struggle to read body language and tone of voice. They might even misinterpret words or phrases.

This leads to misunderstandings and miscommunication.

Secure attachment styles help us feel safe. We feel confident that we can rely on our partners to meet our emotional needs.

Anxious-Avoidant Style

The anxious-avoidant style is characterized by feelings of anxiety, fear, worry, guilt, shame, self-doubt and low self-esteem. They are often quiet, reserved and shy. They avoid conflict and tend to overthink things. This style tends to use avoidance as a coping mechanism.

While there is no one way to communicate effectively with someone with this type of personality, it is important to understand what makes them tick. To help you connect with people and make friends, here are some tips for communicating with others.

1. Don't assume anything.

2. Ask questions.

3. Listen carefully.

4. Show interest.

5. Speak slowly.

Secure Style

There are three types of attachment styles: avoidant, anxious, and ambivalent. Each one represents a different way of relating to others. Insecure people tend to fall somewhere along the spectrum. They might feel comfortable with some relationships while being uncomfortable with others. For example, someone who feels insecure around his mother might be comfortable with his best friend, but he might find himself avoiding her. Someone who feels secure with everyone could easily become clingy with a lover.

The good news is that there are ways to change your attachment style. You don't have to remain stuck in an unhealthy pattern forever. By understanding how each type relates to others, you'll be able to make better choices.

Ways To Create A Secure Attachment Style

Insecure attachment styles can lead us down a path of shame and self-loathing. This often happens because we feel like we are responsible for the way others treat us. If someone doesn't like us, it must mean something about us. Or maybe we blame ourselves for things that aren't even our fault. Either way, insecure attachment leads to low self-esteem and feelings of worthlessness.

Self-forgiveness is important to developing secure attachments. If we don't trust anyone else, we won't let them help us grow. But if we do trust people, we can learn to forgive them when they make mistakes. We can also accept compliments and support from others.

Forgiveness isn't easy, but it's possible. And forgiving ourselves for mistakes helps us become better versions of ourselves. So try to practice forgiveness whenever you think it might be helpful.

Creating a secure attachment style requires putting ourselves first. We have to prioritize ourselves over everything else. This includes spending quality time with friends, family members, and loved ones. It also means taking care of ourselves physically and emotionally.

If we're feeling overwhelmed, we need to give ourselves permission to slow down. Taking breaks from work and social media can help us recharge. And we shouldn't beat ourselves up if we slip up sometimes. Just pick ourselves back up and keep moving forward.

We all have times where we fail to meet our own standards. When those moments happen we can either focus on what went wrong or we can look for ways to improve. Self-compassion is a great tool to use during difficult times. Give yourself some love and remind yourself that you're doing okay.

Improve your nonverbal communication skills

Your body language sends powerful messages. Whether it's how you sit, stand, walk, or gesture during conversation, your body language says a lot about what you think, feel, and want. You might even send subconscious signals to others without realizing it. And whether you realize it or not, your body language affects people around you.

Our emotions are contagious. If you notice yourself feeling stressed, angry, sad, happy, or excited, try to identify where those feelings come from. Are you worried about work? Do you feel guilty about a mistake you made? Is there a reason why you're feeling that way? Try to figure out why you're experiencing that emotion and take steps to manage it.

Mindfulness is a practice that helps you become aware of your thoughts and actions. It teaches you to pay attention to the present moment rather than getting caught up in your mind's wandering. By becoming mindful, you can learn to control your thoughts and emotions.

Practice makes perfect. So start small and build from there. For example, if you see yourself holding your arms stiffly across your chest while talking to another person, try relaxing your hands and shoulders. Or if you find yourself clenching your jaw, try opening your mouth wider. These simple changes can help you improve your nonverbal communication skills.

Body-based interventions

Insecure attachment is one of the most common forms of psychological trauma experienced by children around the world. Children who experience insecure attachment tend to develop negative views about themselves, feel anxious and depressed, and often become stressed and suffer from low self-esteem. These problems can lead to poor physical and emotional health.

The good news is that there are ways to address insecure attachment. A body-based therapy called interoceptive exposure can help people overcome feelings of insecurity. This technique involves learning to recognize emotions and bodily sensations in the present moment, rather than relying on memories of the past or expectations of the future. By doing so, clients learn how to regulate their emotions and improve their ability to cope with stressful situations.

Interoceptive exposure works best when it is combined with cognitive behavioral therapy (CBT). CBT teaches clients to identify thoughts and beliefs that contribute to feeling insecure, and helps them change those patterns of thinking. Interoceptive exposure helps clients understand their bodies' reactions to difficult experiences and allows them to practice accepting what happens without judgment.

Emotional intelligence

Emotional Intelligence is one of those skills that we often take for granted. We are able to read people, empathize, and know how to react accordingly. However, it takes practice to develop this skill. Here's how to boost your EI.

1. Understand what makes you tick

The first step towards developing your EI is understanding yourself better. What do you like doing? Who do you spend most of your time with? Do you prefer to work alone or with others? These questions can help you identify your strengths and weaknesses. For example, if you're good at connecting with people, then you might consider working in sales. If you enjoy being around nature, then perhaps you'd make a great environmentalist. Knowing yourself better will help you figure out what type of job suits you best.

2. Learn about human behavior

Once you've identified your strengths and weaknesses, it's time to learn how to interact with people. You don't always have to be social; however, learning how to communicate effectively can help you connect with others. To start off, try reading books on communication. There are many different types of books that cover different aspects of communicating with others. One book that I recommend is "How to Win Friends & Influence People".

3. Practice empathy

Empathy is another key component to building your EI. By practicing empathy, you become more aware of the feelings of others. When you notice someone struggling with something, ask them how you could help. Or, simply listen to their problems without judgement. Being empathetic will allow you to relate to others.

Develop secure relationships

People who are insecurely attached tend to avoid closeness because it makes them feel vulnerable. They often seek reassurance from others, and they are less likely to make decisions independently. These traits cause people who are insecurely attached to struggle with building trusting relationships. People who are securely attached are comfortable being close to others and making independent choices. They are good at forming friendships and maintaining long-term relationships.

Insecurely attached people are more likely to experience depression, anxiety, and stress than those who are securely attached. For example, research suggests that insecurely attached individuals have higher levels of cortisol, a hormone that increases during times of stress. Cortisol affects how we think and act, especially in stressful situations. High levels of cortisol can lead to feelings of hopelessness, helplessness, and low self-esteem.

Securely attached people are more resilient than those who are insecurely attached. Research indicates that securely attached people are more likely than insecurely attached people to bounce back from negative events. They are also more likely to recover quickly from illness and injury.

Resolve childhood trauma

Childhood trauma affects how we feel and act throughout life. It can cause us to develop physical health issues such as heart disease, diabetes, obesity, high blood pressure, asthma, arthritis, and cancer. And it can affect mental health, including depression, anxiety, posttraumatic stress disorder, bipolar disorder, schizophrenia, attention deficit hyperactivity disorder (ADHD), borderline personality disorder, and suicidal thoughts.

Resolving childhood trauma can help protect against these conditions. When you resolve painful memories associated with early experiences, you change the way you think and behave. You learn to cope better with stressful situations and build healthier relationships. This helps to reduce feelings of loneliness and isolation, improve sleep, and boost energy levels.

Strive towards Secure Attachment

Attachment theory explains how we form relationships with others. We learn about our parents and caregivers early on, and those experiences shape us into adults. This affects how we interact with people in general, including romantic partners. Research shows that there are four primary attachment styles: secure, anxious, avoidant, and disorganized. These styles affect our behavior and emotions in many ways, such as how we approach love and intimacy.

Secure attachment is characterized by trust and safety. People with secure attachments feel safe around others, which makes it easier to open up and explore feelings. They tend to seek out positive interactions with others and avoid negative ones. In addition, they enjoy being close to others because they know they'll be accepted.

Anxious attachment is characterized by fear and insecurity. People with anxious attachments often worry about rejection and abandonment. They're afraid of losing control over themselves and others, and they don't like feeling vulnerable. As a result, they try to protect themselves from harm by avoiding closeness and seeking reassurance.

Avoidant attachment is characterized by anger and hostility. People with avoidant attachments are highly critical of others and dislike showing affection. They prefer to keep distance rather than risk getting hurt.

Disorganized attachment is characterized by confusion and detachment. People with disorganized attachments experience difficulty regulating their emotions and impulses. They aren't able to understand what others want or why they behave the way they do. Disorganization causes problems in social situations, leading to poor interpersonal skills.

Afterword

The most important lesson I learned in my career is that there is no such thing as an average person. Everyone has a story, everyone has a past, everyone has a future. We are all individuals and we are all special.

The study of attachment explains why we do what we do, how we act, and how we feel. It also helps us understand our relationships, our families, and ourselves.

It turns out that the way we relate to each other is deeply rooted in our earliest experiences. These early attachments help shape our sense of self-worth and our ability to form healthy adult relationships.

In short, attachment theory is crucial to understanding human nature.

Understanding attachment theory can help you better understand yourself and those around you. It's helpful for couples who struggle with conflict resolution, for parents who need to understand their children, and for therapists who work with clients.

About the Author

Vanessa Alvarez is an internationally recognized health scientist and author with over 30 years of experience. She studied the effects of mental health on women's bodies, dedicating her life to helping women flourish with natural solutions that are safe and effective.

She was born in Seattle, Washington, but raised in Northern California where she spent most of her childhood exploring the outdoors with her family. Nowadays, when not writing or speaking about her work, you can find her enjoying time by herself with her two cats (Chewy and Bacca) or cooking up a storm at home.

www.ingramcontent.com/pod-product-compliance
Lightning Source LLC
LaVergne TN
LVHW090359210926
848480LV00002B/398